T0294870

Robert Giffen
and the
Giffen Paradox

Robert Giffen
and the
Giffen Paradox

Roger S. Mason

Barnes & Noble Books

Totowa, New Jersey

© Roger S. Mason 1989

All rights reserved. No part of this publication may be
reproduced or transmitted, in any form or by any means,
without the written permission of the publishers.

First published in the USA 1989 by
BARNES & NOBLE BOOKS
81 Adams Drive
Totowa, New Jersey, 07512

ISBN 0–389–20858–2

Printed in Great Britain

Library of Congress Cataloging-in-Publication Data

Mason, Roger S.
  Robert Giffen and the Giffen paradox.

  Bibliography: p.
  Includes index.
  1. Giffen, Robert, Sir, 1837–1910.   I. Title.
HB103.G54M37 1989   338.5'212   88–7862
ISBN 0–389–20858–2

To Sarah, Christopher and,
most of all, Marnie

Contents

Preface

References to Robert Giffen and to the Giffen paradox are found in the majority of books which serve as introductions to economics. Similarly, 'Giffen goods' and 'Giffenesque behaviour' are part of the everyday vocabulary of economists and market analysts. Yet remarkably little is known either about the man or about the paradox which, for many, provides the only real exception to the law of demand.

Robert Giffen's reputation has suffered over the years. When he was knighted in 1895, Alfred Marshall wrote to say how glad he was that the 'Prince of Statisticians has received honour due'. In his day, Giffen had been a confidant of Gladstone and had contributed to the development of statistical ideas and economic thought in late Victorian Britain. Today, however, he is remembered mainly for the economic paradox which bears his name, and even this association has been brought into question in more recent years. Giffen is now seen by many as 'one of those figures encountered frequently in British economics whose not inconsiderable power and prestige appears to be disproportionate to their actual contribution to economic science'.

There is no doubt that Giffen enjoyed great power and prestige for some thirty years and that this added to his influence and reputation. However, his contribution to economics can be too easily dismissed for, using his knowledge of statistics to great effect, he often questioned the new theories of his day and would, when necessary, invite economists to think again. Indeed, he delighted in challenging attempts to produce universal laws and truths and spent the greater part of his life warning against the pitfalls of aggregate analysis and often ridiculous generalisation. In so doing, he was to find few friends among those who were seeking to develop economics into a precise and tidy science, and preoccupation with economic theory did little to help his reputation as a perceptive observer of human nature and of the economics of the real world.

The paradox with which Giffen's name is so closely associated is typically concerned not with aggregate but with disaggregate analysis and describes behaviour to be found only among the very poor, under quite specific economic conditions. While the origins of Giffen's observation have remained obscure beyond the well-known reference in the third edition of Marshall's *Principles of Economics*, the search for evidence linking Giffen directly with the paradox has to date been far from comprehensive. This book offers the first detailed examination of Giffen's life, of that part of his work most directly concerned with the living conditions of the poor and with paradox behaviour itself.

A clearer distinction is also drawn between Giffen's own association with the paradox and the phenomenon as a more general expression of exceptional consumer behaviour. Too great a preoccupation with the Giffen connection obscures the fact that the paradox has been recognised and commented upon by many others, both in Britain and elsewhere, over the past two hundred years, and that it is today an integral part of the theory of inferior goods.

*   *   *

I should like to record my sincere thanks to the many people who have given me their time and expertise in researching this book. In particular, staff of Manchester Central Library, Glasgow University Library, The National Library of Scotland, The British Museum Library and The British Library Newspaper Library gave me every assistance in my search through nineteenth-century archives. My thanks, also, to the London School of Economics, to the British Library of Political and Economic Science for access to 'The Giffen Collection' and to Michael Jackson for his efforts on my behalf in the libraries of London. I am similarly indebted to Ruth Edwards of *The Economist* for sending me a copy of Albert Chapman's memoir. My thanks to the many friends and colleagues at the University of Salford for their constructive criticisms and contributions, and to Jean Waring for typing innumerable drafts with patience and cheerfulness. Above all, I owe an enormous debt of gratitude to my wife Marnie who has been my unpaid research assistant over so many years and without whose help and support this book would never have been written.

Roger S. Mason
University of Salford
December, 1988

CHAPTER 1

Introduction

The law of demand states that, other things being equal, demand for a product will be determined by its price. There is nothing controversial about the law as a general expression of the relationship between value, utility and consumption, for while demand in the market place is certainly influenced by these 'other things' — more particularly, by consumer incomes, by the prices of other products and by individual tastes and preferences — casual observation quickly confirms an inverse relationship between overall demand and price for the great majority of products on offer.

The law of demand, itself derived from the law of diminishing marginal utility, forms a cornerstone of economic theory with respect to aggregate market behaviour. However, it is recognised that where individual or market sector demand is concerned, there are some exceptional circumstances in which demand and price are positively correlated and where perverse demand patterns are produced which do not seem to fall within the law.

One exception arises from the belief, held by consumers, that for most goods there is a strong relationship between price and product quality. In the absence of perfect information or comprehensive product knowledge, price plays an important role in either challenging or confirming customer perceptions with respect to the utility or value of a particular good, and it is often used in this way as an indicator of product worth. Expectations of high quality are reinforced by high asking prices, and vice versa. It therefore follows that if a group of consumers comes to rely on price in this way and, more importantly, is particularly quality-sensitive with respect to a given purchase, then a higher price could persuade it to buy more rather than less of a product.

Whilst this price–quality effect has certainly been shown to
influence demand, it can in fact be explained in a way which
leaves the law of demand intact. For quality-seeking consumers,
it is argued, a higher price effectively changes the nature of a
product, not in a tangible but in a perceptual sense, and it is therefore not legitimate to seek to explain higher levels of demand for a
'new' product as an increase in demand for the 'old'. This explanation, borrowing heavily from the behavioural sciences, avoids
the need to explain in purely economic terms what appears to be
an exception to the law of demand, and it succeeds, at the theoretical level, in leaving the law in good order.

A second apparent exception arises from the phenomenon of
conspicuous consumption. Because the great majority of purchases are made for the personal satisfaction that product
consumption offers to the individual, general theories of
demand and of consumer preference formation are based on the
proposition that goods and services are wanted and purchased
for the direct utility they offer to buyers. However, the conspicuous consumer is concerned primarily with the ostentatious
display of wealth and is motivated by a desire to impress others
with an ability to pay particularly high prices for prestige
products — a form of consumption inspired by the social rather
than by the economic utility of goods. In its pure form,
whenever the consumer is influenced in his decision to buy only
by a wish or need to display purchasing power, the direct utility
of a purchase — that is, its utility in use — is of no interest.
Satisfaction is derived from audience reaction, not to the
positive attributes of the good or service in question but to the
wealth displayed by the purchaser in securing the product for
consumption. Consequently, the cost of purchase — or product
price — becomes the only factor of any significance to such
buyers and the higher the price then the greater the level of
demand becomes.

The conspicuous consumption of goods has been widely
observed, particularly among those who have achieved considerable financial status and who then seek social status
through the display of wealth. The purchase of socially visible
products for purposes of ostentatious display has been seen by
some, therefore, to produce a special case which lies outside
conventional marginal utility theory and which produces a

genuine exception to the law of demand. A more popular approach, however, has been to argue, in much the same way as for the price–quality relationship, that variations in the price of a status good effectively change the product itself — again in a perceptual rather than a physical sense — and that the phenomenon therefore poses no real threat to conventional demand theory.

The law of demand, within its limiting assumptions, is capable of explaining these and other instances of apparently perverse demand (the 'expectations effect' for example) in which price and demand are seen to move in the same direction. However, there is one special case which has posed a greater challenge and which arises because of a paradox which, under certain conditions, can be produced by the effect of price changes on the marginal utility of money.

Consumer incomes clearly play a key part in determining demand for any given commodity. However, income not only provides the means of purchase but the level of income and wealth enjoyed by the consumer also determines the value he places on money. The poorer people are, the greater is the marginal utility of money to them, thus reducing the price that they are willing to pay for any commodity. Conversely, the relatively wealthy consumer considers money to have a far lower marginal utility and is prepared to pay more for the goods he/she wants or needs. It follows, therefore, that changes in money stock simultaneously change the marginal utility of money.

Under the *ceteris paribus* conditions of the law of demand, changes in income are not allowed. However, any purchases made by consumers necessarily reduce their total money stock by the amount of the purchases and raise the marginal utility of money to them. For those whose income or wealth is substantial enough to meet the cost of satisfying general needs in comfort, the marginal effect on money's utility produced by a rise in the price of any necessary good can be considered insignificant. However, among the very poor, the change in the value of money which results from such a price increase will be far more significant.

Under conditions of extreme poverty individuals and families are unable to spend a significant proportion of their incomes on secondary needs and are obliged to concentrate resources on purchasing the essentials of life, foodstuffs in particular. A very large part of total income, moreover, has to be spent on a staple food, typically bread or rice. Given a rise in the price of this staple food, a food which is necessarily 'consuming' a very large part of the total household budget, a special case can arise which produces the major exception to the law of demand. Having no option but to continue purchasing the cheapest staple food, and having experienced, through the price rise, such a marked change in the marginal utility of money, the very poor must necessarily forgo purchases of other, less essential goods with what little resources they have left and increase their consumption of the staple commodity which, notwithstanding the price rise, remains the cheapest food available to them. In this way a rise in price will have produced an *increase* in demand — an increase generated by the negative income effects of the price rise itself.

The process by which the poor may be encouraged to buy more of a staple food in response to a rise in its price is known today as the Giffen paradox, after Sir Robert Giffen, an eminent Victorian statistician, who is credited with first identifying such behaviour. This attribution, however, comes not from any well-documented evidence produced by Giffen in the nineteenth century but from Alfred Marshall, who first made reference to a Giffen 'observation' in the third edition of his *Principles of Economics* (Macmillan, 1895). Marshall himself did not say where or when Giffen had observed the paradox, yet the association with Giffen's name has remained strong. Economists today talk of 'Giffen goods', of 'Giffen effects' and of 'Giffenesque behaviour' in describing similar exceptional market behaviour, and the Giffen paradox is widely referred to as the only legitimate exception to the law of demand.

This book sets out to look more closely at the mysteries which still surround the Giffen paradox. What were the origins of the observation attributed to Giffen by Alfred Marshall? Is the paradox, in any event, nothing more than a contrived theory, or an accurate representation of the behaviour of the poor in times of distress, based on first-hand empirical evidence? And to what extent is the paradox relevant to modern social and economic conditions? The following chapters seek answers to these and other questions.

CHAPTER 2

Retrospect

Book 3, Chapter 6, of the third edition of Alfred Marshall's *Principles of Economics* (1895) deals with the concepts of value and utility, with consumer satisfaction and with the nature of market demand for a variety of goods and services. Here, Marshall argues that although markets react to differences of individual 'sensibility', and to differences of wealth, it is seldom necessary to take account of changes in the purchaser's command of money as there are very few practical problems in which the corrections to be made under this head would be of any importance:

> There are however some exceptions. For instance, as Sir R. Giffen has pointed out, a rise in the price of bread makes so large a drain on the resources of the poorer labouring families and raises so much the marginal utility of money to them, that they are forced to curtail their consumption of meat and the more expensive farinaceous foods: and, bread being still the cheapest food which they can get and will take, they consume more and not less of it. But such cases are rare; when they are met with, each must be treated on its own merits. (p. 208)

Having acknowledged this potential exception to the law of demand, Marshall does not elaborate but moves on to demand prices, making no further reference to the paradox in the book. The paragraph had not, in fact, appeared in either the first or second editions of *Principles* (1890 and 1891 respectively) but it was reprinted in all editions after 1895. While discussion of the paradox was taken no further in *Principles*, however, Marshall was to refer to the subject again on two further occasions.

In a 'Memorandum on the fiscal policy of international trade', written in 1903 and directed at a parliamentary audience, Marshall wrote:

It is indeed, an almost universal rule that a tax on the importation of a commodity lessens its consumption more or less; and the consequent diminution of demand tends to induce foreign producers to offer it on terms which are lower, although not always perceptibly lower. Wheat has conformed to this rule throughout all history, so far as is known, until about forty years ago. But now nearly the whole of the English people can afford to buy as much bread as they want, and yet have money enough left to buy some more expensive foods: and, as Sir R. Giffen seems to have been the first to observe, a rise in the price of bread still leaves bread the cheapest food, which they will consent to eat in any quantity; so that, having to curtail their purchases of more expensive foods, they buy, not less bread than they would have done, but more. (p. 382)

Later, in 1909, he was to defend rather than restate the paradox. In his book *Free Trade in Being*, published in 1908, Russel Rea reproduced correspondence between himself and Professor Pigou which had originally appeared in the columns of *The Westminster Gazette*. In a letter to the *Gazette*, dated 3 September 1908, Rea had written to Pigou:

I should like to suggest to you the elasticity of the British demand (for wheat) might possibly be found to be a positive and not a negative quantity, for I think a rise in the price of wheat would increase rather than decrease the consumption in this country. To all but the poorest class, it would make no difference; if they had to spend more on bread they would spend less on theatres or holidays. The poor, who have a small fixed sum to spend on food, would be obliged to choose between less food and worse food. They would certainly choose the latter, save on their small comforts — meat, eggs, butter etc. — and actually use more of the dearer bread for in England there is no lower grade substitute for wheat bread in common use. (p. 126)

Pigou had replied on 8 September 1908: 'I agree that it is possible that the elasticity of the English demand for wheat may be positive. This certainly used to be the case: but I doubt if it is appreciably the case now' (p. 131). In reviewing Rea's book in the *Economic Journal*, Professor Edgeworth, a noted economist of the day, took issue with the argument that a rise in the price of wheat could increase rather than decrease consumption, and he expressed disbelief on the grounds of 'general experience and commonsense': 'Even the milder statement that the elasticity of demand *may* be positive, although I know it is countenanced by high authority' appears to me so contrary to a priori probability as to require very strong evidence' (p. 105). This criticism provoked Marshall into writing a personal letter to Edgeworth, in 1909, in which he mounted a (distinctly unimpressive) defence of the paradox:

> I have just noticed your review of Rae [sic] in the Ec.J. [xix[1909]]. I don't want to argue. But the hint that a rather rash and random guess has been made by those who suggest that a (moderate) rise in the price of wheat might increase its consumption in England (not generally) provokes me to say that the matter has not been taken quite at random.
>
> When wheat was dear and men were cheap, the estimate of consumption of wheat per head in England was one quarter: now it is, I believe, between 5 and 6 bushels. . . . Ever since I saw Giffen's hint on the subject, I have set myself to compare the amounts of bread (and cake, wheaten biscuits and puddings) eaten at first class dinners in private houses and expensive hotels, with the consumption in middle class houses and second-rate hotels: and again with the consumption in cheap inns, including a low-grade London hotel: and I have watched the baker's supplies to cottages. And I am convinced that the very rich eat less than half as much bread as the poorer classes: the middle class coming midway. This proves nothing conclusively: but it is a fair basis I think, for a surmise as to a probability. (Pigou 1925, pp. 438–9)

These two references to the paradox, made in 1903 and 1909, are of no help in the search for its origins, for on neither occasion does Marshall indicate the source of Giffen's observation or 'hint'. However, they do add something in that the parliamentary memorandum implies that the aggregate demand curve for wheat, and not merely that of the poorer classes, may have a positive slope while the letter to Edgeworth seems to suggest that the paradox holds only for moderate variations in price.

No further references to the paradox were made by Marshall in any of his other writings, and its origins remained obscure. Yet he had been prepared not only to state the paradox in the third edition of *Principles* but also to make use of it in a later parliamentary memorandum, and to defend it in his 1909 correspondence with Edgeworth. Giffen himself, who died in 1910, also never denied the paradox, nor did he ever object to his name being associated with it. Yet the mystery remained — what were the origins of the 1895 statement in *Principles*, and on what evidence had it rested?

The first search of substance into the history of the Giffen paradox was made by George Stigler, the American economist, who published the results of his work in 1947. Stigler did not uncover any firm evidence, although he conceded that his search had been far from exhaustive. He soon became convinced, however, that even if any explicit statement were to come to light, no detailed evidence of paradox behaviour would be found with it. He noted that:

(i) Marshall, who was 'famous for the generosity of his acknowledgements', referred only to Giffen's 'hint';

(ii) in responding to Edgeworth, who was clearly challenging him to reveal his sources, Marshall relied only on personal observations of a very subjective nature and was unable, or unwilling, to quote Giffen directly;

(iii) Giffen himself had continued to treat the demand curve for wheat as negative in slope after 1895.

Whilst Stigler's search for Giffen's statement of the paradox proved fruitless, he was nevertheless persuaded that reference to the paradox in the third edition of *Principles* was, in all probability, a last-minute addition because it stood in bold conflict with the law of demand as defined by Marshall in the same edition: 'There is then one Law of Demand, which is common to all demands, viz. that the greater the amount to be sold, the smaller will be the price at which it will find purchasers. . . . Thus the one universal rule to which the demand curve conforms is that it is inclined negatively throughout the whole of its length' (pp. 175 and 175n).

In the fourth edition of *Principles* (1898) Stigler noted that the law of demand was stated more cautiously: 'There is then one general Law of Demand, viz. that the greater the amount to be sold, the smaller the price at which it will find purchasers' (p. 174). This change of emphasis could well have been influenced by Marshall's recognition of the paradox. However, the footnote stating a universal law of negative slope persisted in all later editions, thus significantly weakening the argument that the paradox had been entered in the third edition so hastily that its consequence for other parts of the text had been necessarily ignored.

Stigler's unsuccessful search for Giffen's statement of the

paradox, and his pessimism as to whether any evidence of such behaviour did indeed exist, prompted a response from Cambridge University. Writing in the same journal, Prest (1948) suggested that the source of the paradox could be found in the following passage of a memorandum written by Giffen, which appeared as an appendix to the *Final Report of the Royal Commission on Agricultural Depression* (1897):

> It may be suggested that as the fall in (the price of) cereals cannot be ascribed to an excessive growth of the production of the cereals themselves, it must be ascribed, seeing that there has been a great increase of the resources of the consuming peoples themselves, to a diminution of demand arising from various causes. What can be these causes? Why do people as they grow rich consume less wheat etc. instead of more? The answer to the last question is to be found, I think, in an examination of the figures as to livestock. . . . People consume less cereals per head because, with their increase of resources, they consume more meat, which *pro tanto* displaces the cereals. (Cmnd. 8541, Appendix 5)

At first sight, this could not have been the source of the paradox statement as it was included in documents published in 1897, some two years after publication of the third edition of *Principles*. However, Prest pointed out that the memorandum itself was dated '8.1.95' and could therefore have been seen by Marshall before committing the third edition of his book to print. Prest went on to argue that this afforded an a-priori reason for believing that the quotation was indeed the origin of Marshall's paragraph in *Principles*.

Prest's claim to have found the paradox drew an immediate response from Stigler (1948):

> The passage of Giffen's memorandum in which Mr Prest finds the paradox does not contain it, as the reader should verify. And if he turns to the original — a two-page affair plus some statistical tables on agricultural outputs (but not prices) — he will find no reason for reading the paradox into the passage. The entire discussion relates to the European-populated countries, not to England. Giffen apparently argues — he is far from clear — that the increased cheapness of meat has reduced the demand (curve) for cereals. There is no reference to working (or income) classes or to the cost of wheat being a larger proportion of a poor man's budget. All that one can find is a statement of the negative income elasticity of wheat. And that is simply not enough. (p. 61)

Stigler insisted that the Giffen paradox was more than a
restatement of the existence of so-called 'inferior' goods and
rightly challenged Prest's claim to have found the paradox,
when in fact he had only produced a statement of the relative
inferiority of wheat to meat. Prest's reference to the Royal
Commission on Agricultural Depression, however, prompted
Stigler to read Giffen's evidence, and he noted that in April 1894
Giffen had been asked by a Commission member, John Shaw-
Lefevre: 'I do not know whether you have examined the figures
of the prices of wheat and the results per acre of land in
England. I think it showed that 1879 was the first time when the
prices of wheat did not rise in proportion to the deficiency of
the harvest?' Stigler felt that this question came fairly close to
asking 'Is there a Giffen paradox, Giffen?' Giffen, however, had
replied:

> I cannot say that I observed that in particular, because I think about
> that time the question of the deficiency of the English harvest was
> becoming less and less important, owing to the intercommunication
> with foreign countries and the diminution of the crop of wheat in this
> country itself in proportion to the total consumption. I should not
> like to go into that without examining it. (Minutes of Evidence II,
> C-7400-II, p. 139)

Stigler concluded that Giffen had 'refused an invitation to state
the paradox which, some eighteen months later, Marshall
attributed to him'. The 1894 testimony also convinced Stigler
that Giffen either had no evidence of the paradox or was,
perhaps, unaware that he had ever produced any: 'One may
also entertain strong doubts that Giffen, who was not a subtle
analyst, ever realised that he had hinted the paradox, and it
would probably be more just (to him as well as to Marshall) to
call it "Marshall's Paradox"' (Stigler 1948, p. 62).

In so far as the 'hint' itself was concerned, Stigler was persuaded that this would be found to predate 1893. In support of
this claim, he referred again to Marshall's 1909 correspondence
with Edgeworth, in which Marshall had stated that, having seen
Giffen's hint, he had set about comparing the amounts of bread
consumed in various social classes. Stigler pointed out that
Marshall had, in fact, reported on some research into patterns of
bread consumption while discussing a paper published by

Higgs in 1893, a fact which therefore seemed to put Giffen's observation before that date. (This argument is unconvincing: Marshall's 1893 'research' was subjective, negligible and unrelated to the paradox.)

Both Stigler and Prest had also looked at the wider issue of whether any empirical evidence could be found which would validate the paradox quite independently of any link with Giffen. To this end, Stigler firstly carried out a study of relevant time-series data listing per-capita wheat consumption and wheat prices over the period 1889–1904 in order to test the hypothesis that upward movements in price had in fact increased consumption. The results of this study did not in any way confirm the existence of the paradox, although Stigler conceded that if the paradox did indeed relate only to working-class consumption of wheat, it would not be possible to detect such behaviour within aggregate statistical data. Stigler's second approach was to examine working-class family budgets alone in order to look for paradox behaviour among the more deprived, with a view to isolating these statistics from other social and economic groups. However, 1889 and 1904 Board of Trade studies into urban working-class family incomes and expenditure on bread and flour again revealed no evidence of the paradox. There was a small and positive income elasticity in the 1904 data, and although the earlier report did appear to show a large negative income elasticity for wheat in the lowest income classes it was based on a sample of only 34 families.

Prest was critical of Stigler's search for empirical evidence. The paradox, he argued, related specifically to bread whereas Stigler's time-series analyses referred to wheat consumption. Furthermore, no allowance had been made for income variations, prices of substitutes or a time trend. Emphasising the weakness of aggregate data, Prest pointed out not only that it was impossible to obtain accurate time-series data for working-class consumption of bread but also that the paradox referred specifically to the poorer labouring classes within the working class itself, so creating an even more difficult task for the statistical researcher. With respect to family budgets, Prest again questioned the data which had been used by Stigler, but conceded that in later studies carried out in 1905 and in 1937–8 there was evidence to suggest some negative income elasticity of demand for bread. Prest, however, felt that these studies fell far short of providing sufficient evidence to confirm the existence of the paradox.

* * *

Both the search for Giffen's original statement, or 'hint', and work into the separate but related issue of whether any evidence exists to support the claim that such behaviour can occur have been remarkably unproductive. Despite the work of Stigler and Prest, we are no nearer today to locating the source of any statement, with Stigler concluding that in all probability Giffen never said or wrote it or, at the very least, was unaware that he had done so. We do not know the extent of Stigler's research into Giffen's written work and into his evidence on Select Committees and Commissions, but he himself did not make any claim that the research had been exhaustive. Giffen was a prolific author and held an important post at the Board of Trade for some twenty years, during which time he was involved with the preparation and publication of numerous reports. On his own admission, Stigler had not undertaken any comprehensive examination of this material. Prest, mistakenly believing that he had found the paradox statement, can be assumed to have carried out an even less intensive search.

As the paradox first appears in the third edition of Marshall's *Principles*, it is tempting to believe that any search should concentrate on that period of time which elapsed between publication of the second and third editions of the book. Prest and Stigler clearly focused their attention here. However, the search needs to be far more extensive. There is no reason to suppose that Giffen's observation was not made much earlier, and this view is strengthened when it is recognised that the social and economic conditions best suited to producing paradox behaviour were to be found well before 1890, and that Giffen was writing on social and economic matters as early as 1860.

With regard to the search for evidence of paradox behaviour, no work of substance has been carried out. The paradox can never emerge from aggregate statistical returns on bread prices and consumption, for, as Stigler and Prest realised, only disaggregated data can offer information on one particular sector of the working class. Similarly, budget studies which relate income to expenditure on bread are of no value if they do not include information on the price of bread and on any changes in the price of a loaf which occur over the period to which the budget data relate. This is simply because the paradox occurs as a response to increases in the price of bread, and, without details of such price changes, no investigation of family budgets can hope to identify instances of such exceptional consumer behaviour.

In searching for empirical evidence of the paradox, pre-occupation with the 1890s and with the first decade of the twentieth century is surely misplaced. By this time, as we shall see, the conditions necessary to produce the paradox were becoming more difficult to find in Britain. In particular, the price of bread, though still important, had been falling steadily in real terms since 1890 and was no longer of such overwhelming importance in the budgets of the poor. Expenditure on bread, expressed as a percentage of weekly income, fell significantly, giving the poor more room for manoeuvre and reducing their dependence on the loaf as the family's staple food. Bread, in short, was losing some of its social and economic significance — a fact signalled by the end of bread riots and by a corresponding decline in political sensitivity to wheat harvests and to the price of a loaf.

A further reason for examining earlier periods of the nine-teenth century in the search for evidence of the paradox comes, not unnaturally, from a wish to link any evidence which Giffen himself may have seen and recorded to the statement made by Marshall in 1895. No search for empirical evidence has been carried out over the period which covered the earlier part of Giffen's working life, and it is possible — even probable — that the paradox relates to events which took place during this time. Again, the conditions which prevailed earlier in the Victorian age were far more conducive to paradox behaviour than those found during the last decade of the century.

If we are to learn more about Giffen's paradox and to have any realistic chance of identifying the source of the statement which appeared in 1895 we need to know more of the background, career and work of Robert Giffen himself. At the same time, the search for the paradox has to proceed within a far wider time frame than hitherto has been the case. Giffen's articles and speeches span more than forty years and need to be examined in greater detail. And if evidence of such exceptional consumer behaviour is not to be found within these records, then the work of Giffen's contemporaries may provide new and valuable information.

References

Edgeworth, F.Y. (1909) 'Review of *Free Trade in Being*' (by Russel Rea), *Economic Journal*, Vol. 19, pp. 102–6.

Higgs, H. (1893) 'Workmen's budgets', *Journal of the Royal Statistical Society*, Vol. 56, pp. 225–85. 'Comment', pp. 286–8.

Marshall, A. (1895) Principles of Economics (3rd edn), Macmillan.

Marshall, A. (1903) 'Memorandum on the fiscal policy of international trade', in J.M. Keynes (ed.) (1926) *Official Papers by Alfred Marshall,* Macmillan. The Memorandum was revised for publication in 1909.

Pigou, A.C. (ed.) (1925) *Memorials of Alfred Marshall*, Macmillan.

Prest, A.R. (1948) 'Notes on the history of the Giffen paradox: comment', *Journal of Political Economy*, Vol. 56 (February), pp. 58–60.

Rea, R. (1908) *Free Trade in Being*, Macmillan.

Stigler, G.J. (1947) 'Notes on the history of the Giffen paradox', *Journal of Political Economy*, Vol. 55 (April), pp. 152–6.

Stigler, G.J. (1948) 'A reply', *Journal of Political Economy*, Vol. 56 (February), pp. 61–2.

──────────────

CHAPTER 3

Robert Giffen

By the time of his death, in 1910, Sir Robert Giffen had established his reputation as a statistician and as an unconventional, but respected, political economist. The many obituaries which appeared at the time acknowledged the great esteem in which he had been held — both in public and private life — and paid tribute to the width and depth of his achievements.

Giffen's successful career had been all the more remarkable in that he was, for the most part, a self-made man. He was born in 1837 in Strathaven, Lanarkshire, the son of a village grocer, and his boyhood was spent in relatively humble surroundings. Educated at the village school, he showed an early aptitude for journalism by contributing articles to the local newspaper but, upon leaving school at thirteen, he was apprenticed to a solicitor's clerk and spent much of his time in Glasgow. It was during this period (1850–7) that he also attended two sessions at Glasgow University. Subsequently, he spent two years in a commercial house but in 1860 decided to pursue a career in journalism and joined the *Stirling Journal* as reporter and sub-editor.

In 1862 he travelled south to London, becoming sub-editor of the *Globe* — not a conservative newspaper at that time but little more than a vehicle for the views of Lord Palmerston in the closing period of his life. Four years later, and married to Isabella McEwen of Glasgow, he moved on as assistant editor of the liberal *Daily News* which, in 1869, was to take in the more radical and Cobdenite *Morning Star*. He also took on other responsibilities as assistant editor of the *Fortnightly Review* and became a regular contributor to the *Spectator* and other journals, including the *Saturday Review*.

In 1867 Giffen wrote his first major article — on the reduction of the National Debt — and that same year he joined the Statistical Society, with which he was to form a very close association over the coming years, culminating in his Presidency of the Society in 1882–4. In 1868 he was appointed assistant editor of *The Economist*, later becoming city editor (1870–6) and a principal contributor under the editorship of Walter Bagehot, a man who was to have a significant influence on Giffen's journalistic style. The year 1868 also saw Giffen invited to help J.J. (later Lord) Goschen, President of the Poor Law Board, with a historical retrospect and statistics for the Local Taxation Report to the Treasury. This was a controversial decision at the time but one which was vindicated on publication of the Report, an event which was to lay the foundations of Giffen's reputation as a statistician.[1]

By 1873 Giffen was city editor not only of *The Economist* but also of the *Daily News*, a newspaper whose prestige had been greatly enhanced by its coverage of the Franco-German War. Three years later he accepted an invitation to become editor of the *Journal of the Statistical Society*, having been a member of the journal's council since 1872.

Giffen was, at this point, developing two parallel reputations: one as a newspaper journalist and editor, the other as a highly competent statistician. It was becoming increasingly obvious that a choice would have to be made between the two careers. In 1876 he was offered the appointment of Chief of the Statistical Department and Comptroller of Corn Returns at the Board of Trade and decided to accept, thus choosing the Civil Service in preference to journalism. On taking up his new position, he severed all official connections with *The Economist* and the *Daily News*. However, in 1877 Walter Bagehot died suddenly, leaving vacant the editorship of *The Economist*. It was rumoured at the time that Giffen, having worked closely with Bagehot for so many years, was interested in the editorship and was very disappointed not to be offered the post. It was perhaps no coincidence, therefore, that one year later, in 1878, he was instrumental in founding *The Statist*, a journal which was to become *The Economist*'s main rival.[2]

As Chief of the Board of Trade Statistical Department, Giffen was primarily responsible for the compilation and publication of UK trade and agricultural statistics and for improving methods of data collection. His arrival at the Board of Trade in 1876 also heralded the start of many appearances before Select Committees and Royal Commissions. His grasp of detail, appreciation of economic history and his access to official statistics made him a valuable witness to such enquiries, although his contributions were often contentious and sometimes provocative. He rarely offered evidence which could not be substantiated by statistical data, but his appearances became more controversial when he was invited to interpret the research.

Although he had chosen a career within the Civil Service, Giffen did not sever all links with journalism, and his easy access to the press was to increase his power and influence in the years to come. In 1877 he had published his first book on Stock Exchange Securities. Other books and articles were to follow, for upon entering the Civil Service he had negotiated a special dispensation to continue writing independently. He became a frequent contributor to the letters page of *The Times* and used this as a channel to answer his critics. Several of these letters were subsequently to form the basis of extended articles published in academic journals and magazines.

In 1881 his strong links with the press nearly forced his resignation from the Board of Trade. Having agreed to assist the city desk of *The Times* by contributing 'anonymously' to a regular and somewhat controversial feature on trade and finance, his duties at the Board of Trade were temporarily suspended. Whilst his possible resignation became a matter for discussion, this in fact never took place. Indeed, in 1882 his power at the Board increased when, under Gladstone's premiership, the Statistical Department was merged with a reformed Commercial Department and Giffen took responsibility for both as Assistant Secretary. His contributions to the *Times* articles ended in 1884, however, shortly after he had severed his official connection with *The Statist*.

While some of Giffen's links with journalism were being questioned, his association with the Statistical Society had continued to flourish. He remained as editor of the Society's prestigious journal and was elected President in 1882. The frequent meetings and debates of the Society were increasingly attracting the best minds of the day on matters of statistics and political economy and gave Giffen the opportunity to reach a wide and knowledgeable audience.

Throughout the 1880s, Giffen's stature and prestige increased. In 1883 the President of the Board of Trade, Joseph Chamberlain, officially acknowledged Giffen as the real author of the bankruptcy legislation carried through Parliament in 1882. In 1884 he was awarded an honorary degree by Glasgow University. Following on the work of G.R. Porter, the founder of the Board of Trade Official Statistics, and of Richard Valpy, who instituted the official abstracts relating to the United Kingdom, the Colonies and foreign countries, Giffen greatly improved methods of data collection and interpretation and revised the presentation of official tables. He was particularly successful in suggesting new ways of attacking statistical problems relating to the measurement of national income, and he greatly improved the quantity and quality of relevant data. He never restricted himself to his essential duties and was always prepared to interpret statistical evidence which came before him. He wrote several papers relating to the taxation of Ireland, including a series of letters to *The Statist* under the pseudonym 'Economist'. His two papers on the progress of the working classes, published in 1883 and 1886, attracted national attention. He launched a fierce defence of free trade as the old protectionist arguments were heard again, delivering an impressive address from the President's Chair of the Economic and Statistical Section of the British Association, assembled in Manchester in 1887. On all these subjects, Giffen was seen 'to have a natural aptitude for pricking all sorts of sensational bubbles, and evidently took pleasure in pouring a cold douche of facts and figures on all perfervid oratory that seemed to him wrongly directed' (*Glasgow Herald*).

In 1885 Giffen helped to found the International Statistical Institute in London. Such was his reputation by this time that his advice was sought on many home and overseas affairs. In 1887 he was invited to join the prestigious Monetary Committee of the British Association, whose purpose was to investigate the best methods of ascertaining and measuring variations in the value of the monetary standard.[3] By the end of the decade, Giffen's reputation as a statistician of eminence was secure. In the late 1880s and early 1890s his work at the Board of Trade centred around the compilation of statistics for use at the Labour Commission, which sat from 1892–4 and to which Giffen was to give evidence. The Bureau of Labour Statistics had been constituted within the Board of Trade since 1886, and remained there even after the setting up of a new Department of Labour in 1893.[4] Giffen, who was required to give the Bureau the time and resources necessary to its efficient operation, complained that preoccupation with the Commission's needs within the Board of Trade had, in fact, diverted too much time and effort away from other equally important projects.

In 1893 Giffen became a member of the Royal Commission on Agriculture, whose final report appeared in 1897. In 1895 publication of his long-awaited *Blue Book* on the wages of the manual labouring classes completed a series of similar reports on wages in the principal trades of the United Kingdom. The *Blue Book* itself was controversial and promoted much public attention.

Away from the Board of Trade, Giffen was a founder member of the Royal Economic Society (1890) and gave up the editorship of the *Journal of the* [now] *Royal Statistical Society* in 1891 only to help found the *Economic Journal* the following year. Throughout the 1890s, he joined in the debate on bimetallism. A convinced monometallist, he used his influence, both inside and outside the Civil Service, to make the case against bimetallism; so successful was he, according to *The Economist*, that a Giffen letter to *The Times* in 1897 'effectively snuffed out bimetallism as a practical project for this country'.

Public recognition of Giffen's work came first in 1891, when he was awarded the CB (Civil). In 1892 he was elected a Fellow of the Royal Society and two years later received the Guy Medal of the Royal Statistical Society. Finally, in 1895, he was knighted — an honour regarded by many as long overdue. In 1896, one year after the death of his first wife, Giffen married Margaret Ann Wood, daughter of an Aberdeen businessman. Soon after, with his health failing, he chose to take early retirement and left the Board of Trade in September 1897, so bringing to an end 21 years of prominent public service.

In retirement, freed from the demands of office, he began to extend his range of interests, publishing books and articles on a wide variety of subjects. He became a frequent contributor to the *Economic Journal*, the *Nineteenth Century* and the *Contemporary Review* and remained active within the Royal Statistical Society. Now an even more prolific contributor to the letters page of *The Times*, he presented papers to various Chambers of Commerce, to the Royal Colonial Institute and to the Institute of Bankers, among others, and many of these papers were later to be included in his book *Economic Inquiries and Studies* (George Bell & Sons, 1904). He also entered into wide-ranging correspondence with many personalities of the day and clearly did not hesitate to offer his opinion on current statistical, economic and political issues. As a distinguished former civil servant, his presence at dinners and banquets was much sought after, and Giffen took such opportunities to make it clear that he had retired only from the Board of Trade and not from the political and economic stage.

He remained controversial to the end. The 1906 Liberal Government, he felt, had betrayed fundamental Liberal principles. By 1909, his disillusionment with the party he had supported all his life was complete, and he announced his intention of voting Unionist, preferring the tariff reform of the latter to the 'socialism' of Lloyd George's budget. 'We who are Free Traders', he wrote, 'have been "sold" by the Government. We have learnt our lesson, and never again can we trust a party which pretends to be Free Trade and uses its power to destroy institutions which we consider vital to the national welfare.'

Giffen's political disillusionment was not to worry him for long. In April 1910, on one of his frequent visits back to Scotland, he died suddenly and unexpectedly at the Lovat Arms Hotel in Fort Augustus. He was buried in his home town of Strathaven at a private ceremony attended by a few close friends.

* * *

Whilst any review of Giffen's career serves to demonstrate the magnitude of his achievements, it is also important to know something more of the man himself and of the formative years which shaped his values and beliefs. The obituaries which appeared at the time of his death revealed much of Giffen's character and personality. He was seen as kind and considerate, yet lacking in sentimentality, a man of great common sense who was a glutton for work, and an impressive but not eloquent speaker — at his best in private conversation. He was fortunate to have a highly retentive memory, and throughout his working life he kept no diary and took no notes. Outside work, his interests lay in chess and in literature. *The Times* talks of his wide general reading and of his finely cultivated taste in history, memoirs, fiction and poetry — indeed, as a boy he had wanted to be a poet himself and had written several poems in his earlier years.

Politically, he was a moderate liberal for the greater part of his life. He was described as a 'sane imperialist and a convinced Free Trader' with a passionate dislike of both protectionism and socialism. His commitment to free trade was evident throughout his working life — a commitment which made him many enemies both at the Board of Trade and on Royal Commissions, where he took delight in showing the fair traders, and particularly the wealthy landowners, to be greedy and uncaring.

As a statistician and writer on matters of political economy he had a special talent for getting to the heart of a mass of statistics, and his analyses were invariably based on inductive logic. The *Economic Journal* credited him with an arithmetical sense which almost amounted to genius whilst having little or no knowledge of mathematical or statistical theory. He certainly popularised the use of statistics through his journalistic flair and so gained a reputation, with the general public, as one of the best informed and most able statisticians of his day.

On economic matters, he was Ricardian and staunchly *laissez-faire*, but the quality of his work is often understated today. He was among the first to analyse the workings of the quantity theory of money and the role played by the rate of interest, and his ideas certainly seem to have had a great deal of influence on Alfred Marshall. Most of all, however, he is remembered for his refusal to accept economic theories at face value, believing that many economists had a tendency to carry their theories too far at the expense of practical observation and application. In later years, he delighted in being seen as 'the *bête noire* of economic quacks and fanatics' (*Glasgow Herald*).

In many ways, therefore, Robert Giffen was neither conformist nor conventional. In their final tribute to him, the *Journal of the Royal Statistical Society* — with which he had been closely associated for over forty years — described him, perhaps most accurately, as follows:

> Born one of the people and brought up among radical if not democratic surroundings, he became in middle and later life essentially an aristocrat in its original and proper sense, having perhaps a too high opinion of brain and intellect in all callings and something nearly approaching contempt for mediocracy and work of a poor class. But whatever his opinions on any subject, his courtesy and geniality, combined with his love of a paradox, and his unconventional views, made him excellent company. (May 1910, p. 533)

Giffen had certainly been 'born one of the people', and his early life in Strathaven was far from privileged. The town's wealth lay largely in the hands of the Duke of Hamilton who owned several thousand acres of land within the parish — land which was reserved for sheep-rearing and grouse shooting. As a grocer's son in the Hungry Forties, Giffen would have seen, at first hand, the impact of economic distress on the wealth of the town and the ways in which this affected his father's trade.

Strathaven would also have introduced the young Giffen to radical politics. The town gained an early reputation for the strength of its opposition to the Corn Laws. As early as 1815, a meeting was held in the Relief Church demanding repeal of the Laws, and discontent continued to grow among the town's several hundred weavers over the years which followed. The so-called Strathaven Radicals also played a significant role in the Scottish Insurrection of 1820. Led by James Wilson, they took part in the abortive march on Glasgow, only to see the entire operation fail as quickly as it had begun. Wilson was subsequently arrested, found guilty of treason and hanged in Glasgow that same year. To the people of Strathaven, however, he was seen as a martyr who had given his life in the cause of social justice. His body was taken back to Strathaven for an honoured but secret burial in the parish churchyard only a few yards from his own house. Some years later, a monument to his memory was erected in the churchyard, paid for by public subscription, not only to honour Wilson but also to confirm and reinforce the continuing radicalism of the small community.

Strathaven's radicalism persisted throughout the 1840s and 1850s. In such an atmosphere it is hardly surprising that Giffen was to develop those attitudes which characterised his work over the years to come. First-hand observations of the harsh realities of the Corn Laws convinced him at an early age of the necessity for free trade, a conviction he held until his death. Throughout his life he was to display a particular prejudice against the land-owning interest, holding them largely responsible for the plight of the labouring classes, not only in Strathaven but throughout the country. His early writings on taxation and on other economic matters always identified with the needs of the poor and with the political necessity to ensure that social justice was seen to be done. However, he was openly sceptical as to whether 'a Parliament of landowners' could ever be trusted to enact the necessary legislation. Given these values and beliefs, it is a measure of Giffen's ambition and ability that he was able to rise so high within the Victorian establishment.

His early years spent as a journalist, coupled with a career at the Board of Trade which gave him access to statistical data from many separate sources, allowed Robert Giffen an insight into social and economic realities which was often denied to others. Moreover, his Scottish background and experiences gave him an understanding of working-class values and aspirations which were often disregarded by contemporary economists and political commentators. No lover of dogma, and unrestricted by any formal economic education, Giffen's 'love of a paradox', remarked upon by the Royal Statistical Society, comes as no surprise.

Notes

1. The Report, published in March 1871, was concerned 'with the progressive increase of local taxation and the proportion of burden borne by classes of real property'. Goschen acknowledged Giffen's contribution in a footnote: 'I have pleasure in expressing my acknowledgements of the valuable assistance which Mr Robert Giffen has rendered me in the collection of historical materials and in the compilation of the various tables contained in the appendices.' The *Journal of the Statistical Society* later expressed a belief that Giffen's work

was of such quality that it prepared the way for his subsequent appointment at the Board of Trade.

2. Albert Chapman, a clerk on *The Economist* who had joined the staff in 1898, wrote in a memoir, dated 1942: 'I heard on very good authority from a friend of Giffen's that Robert Giffen was very disappointed that he did not secure the Editorship of *The Economist* and, as a solace, that he assisted in or was instrumental in the foundation of *The Statist* which first appeared in 1878. If this story is true Robert Giffen must have felt in his heart that he stood a chance of securing the Editorship whenever it might fall vacant. It was not to be, however, and the disappointment may have profoundly affected his future career.'

3. Committee members included Professors Edgeworth and Marshall, both of whom were later to be involved in the debate over the Giffen paradox.

4. Giffen was, in fact, asked to head the new Labour Department but declined.

CHAPTER 4

Giffen and the Poor

In one of his earliest articles, written in 1867, Robert Giffen pointed to the dramatic rise in living standards which had been brought about over the preceding twenty years. The abolition of the Corn Laws in 1846 had, in his opinion, produced substantial improvements for the working classes, who were now enjoying a standard of living which would have been unrecognisable to their fathers and grandfathers. Giffen estimated that in 1867 the country was three times wealthier than fifty years before, an advance which had for the most part taken place since 1845. At the same time, he was in no doubt where the major benefits had fallen:

> It has to be taken into account besides that the classes whose wealth has increased most are probably not the number, comparatively small, who pay income tax, but the great masses of people, among whom the general average of comfort has notoriously advanced, so that the general wealth may have increased in much greater ratio than the portion affected by the income tax. (p. 267)

The main thrust of the article was to argue that the rich should shoulder the burden of reducing the National Debt in order to leave the working classes with the gains for which they had fought for so many years. However, in a paper which appeared later that same year in the *Fortnightly Review*, Giffen not only expressed doubts about the willingness of Parliament to impose any significant tax burdens upon the rich but also appeared to qualify his opinion as to the new 'prosperity' of the masses. Looking at the possibility of new indirect taxes being placed on food and other basic goods, he observed:

> . . . there are many working men whose incomes are less than the

minimum, so that to tax their comforts or poor luxuries is really to cripple them in the performance of their first duty, and embitter still further the wretchedness of their lives. . . . Let any one calculate how much the brute necessaries of life, even of course quality cost, how much must be spent by the poorest for wretched clothing and shelter, and he must acknowledge that, although working men contrive to exist on smaller sums, they do not maintain life and health in a way that can be considered satisfactory either to themselves or the community. Their living is little better than a sort of death in life. (p. 716)

Anticipating arguments that the working classes, nevertheless, always found it possible to spend money on alcohol and on other strictly non-essential goods, he added:

. . . much of what is coldly condemned as waste is in grim reality an expenditure on the medicine of misery, not to be summarily pronounced injudicious by those who have never felt what life is down filthy courts and in crowded ill-ventilated rooms; conditions which almost force the unfortunate to seek relief in gin and beer. The remedy may be worse than the disease, but the gin and beer taken in this way are in some sense necessary to make life endurable, though the expense trenches on the minimum required for its support. It is too often only a choice of evils for the poor. (p. 722)

Beer, tea and sugar were seen by Giffen as 'absolute necessaries of life' to the working person, forced to live in the most deprived social and economic conditions. At the same time, he had little faith in Parliament's commitment to keep taxes on such products as low as possible, preferring to believe that a Government dominated by landowners and the ruling classes would act in ways unfavourable to the interests of the working classes if and when these interests conflicted with their own.

For many years, after 1870, Giffen's journal articles make little reference to the life and conditions of the working classes. A convinced free trader, he believed that the 1870s had brought about a significant improvement in living standards. In 1879, he gave an address to the Statistical Society, in which he discussed the fall in commodity prices between 1873 and 1879. One reason for this fall was, he argued, the three bad harvests of 1875–7, but he also noted that the crop failures had *not* caused the price of bread to rise:

Now perhaps, we are only beginning to appreciate how bad the harvests were in this country for the three years before 1878. The fact that the great rise in the price of wheat and bread which was formerly considered the worst effect of a bad harvest, and the most powerful cause of the succeeding depression, has not been observed in recent years, helped to blind businessmen to the actual deficiency. But the deficiency was most serious. The wheat harvest to begin with was undoubtedly most deficient . . . by one-fourth as compared with the average, and much more of course as compared with a good year for three years running. The usual rise in wheat and bread has not followed, owing to the very fact that the home yield is now less important than the aggregate foreign importations, but other effects of a deficient harvest must have ensued. (pp. 46–7)

There is no doubt that, throughout the 1870s, cheap imports of foreign wheat were removing any fears of higher bread prices resulting from failures of the UK harvest. To Giffen, this guarantee of cheap wheat and bread was total justification for the earlier abolition of the Corn Laws and for the free-trade policies to which he was so strongly committed. With bread prices under control, the suffering of many millions of poorer people was being alleviated, and the grinding poverty and bread riots of the recent past could soon be forgotten.

Whilst Giffen welcomed the wheat imports which were effectively introducing a new era of cheaper food, the landowning interests in Britain were far from enthusiastic. Demands for new tariff protection were becoming increasingly strident as wheat farmers found their ability to control market prices was more and more limited. By 1879, the movement against free trade was gaining rapid momentum and the case for protection was being canvassed both inside and outside Parliament. Giffen was forced to respond. His position as a senior civil servant made it difficult for him to take up an overtly political stance, but writing under the pseudonym 'Economist' he published a pamphlet (1879b) in which he attacked the arguments of the protectionists.

The agricultural lobby was arguing that the best interests of British manufacturing industry would be served if a substantial tax were to be put on imports of American corn. Giffen, however, saw this, quite rightly, as nothing more than an attempt to put money back into the pockets of the landowners rather than to help the manufacturing sector, and was scathing in his attack on the real beneficiaries of such a policy. Agriculture, the business 'specially petted and pampered by the

State', would, he argued, be 'flooded with candidates', and the tax would produce massive rises in land rents. The prospect of increased prosperity for the landowners clearly appalled him:

> As a class they are already wealthy and surrounded by all the necessaries and luxuries which seem to be demanded for their comfort and enjoyment. If you make them richer there are certain things which they are most likely to do with their money. I will enumerate a few of them. Game preserves will be extended and the cultivation of game will be increased. There will be more hunting, and a greater number of expensive hunters in the stables. There will be an increase in the existing studs, and a larger number of racehorses. Farms will be laid into parks. The larger and the richer landowners will buy up at any price the smaller estates to add to their own grandeur, whereby the possession of land will become a greater monopoly than ever. (pp. 16–17)

Giffen's opposition to any reintroduction of import duties on wheat was restated no less forcefully in his evidence to the 1881–2 Royal Commission on Agriculture. Here, he was at pains to point out that domestic agricultural depression, however regrettable, had to be seen in a wider context. In particular, the benefits to the consumer which resulted when substantial imports of wheat were allowed to offset shortfalls in home production could never be overlooked. Giffen was adamant that no cure for an ailing domestic agriculture should be found at the expense of the poor and that taxes on wheat imports were for this reason totally unacceptable.

Giffen's defence of free trade was to continue for much of his life, but the mid-1880s were the years in which he was to concern himself most directly with the conditions and living standards of the poor. On 20 November 1883, Giffen gave his inaugural address as President of the Statistical Society on 'The Progress of the Working Classes in the Last Half Century'. The paper had clearly political overtones:

> In asking you . . . to look for a little at what statistics tell us of the progress of the great masses of the nation, I feel I am selecting a subject which is connected with the special history of the Society. That it happens for the moment to be attracting a considerable amount of popular attention in connection with sensational politics and sociology, with agitations for land nationalisation and collectivism among pretended representatives of the working classes, is an

additional reason for our not neglecting this question; but it is a question to which the Society has a primary claim, and which the authors of the agitations I have referred to would have done well to study from the statistical point of view. (pp. 595–6)

The intention of the speech was to make an informed comparison between the living conditions of the working classes in the 1830s and those of the 1880s. His first problem, however, was to recognise the lack of statistical information on which such a comparison could be made:

There are two or three ways in which statistics may throw light on such a question as I have put forward. The first and most direct is to see what records there are of the money earnings of the masses now and fifty years ago, ascertain whether they have increased or diminished, and then compare them with the rise or fall in the prices of the chief articles which the masses consume. . . . In investigating such records, however, we have to recognise that the ideal mode of answering the question is not yet possible. . . . In the absence of such statements (of aggregate annual earnings) all that can be done is to compare what appear to be the average wage of large groups of the working classes. If it is found that the changes in the money wages of such groups are in the same direction, or almost all in the same direction, then there would be sufficient reason for believing that similar changes had occurred throughout the entire mass. (p. 596)

Giffen proceeded on this basis. Referring to data on the wages of carpenters, bricklayers, weavers and other groups — both in the 1820s and 1830s, and in the 1880s — he concluded that there had been an enormous apparent rise in money wages ranging from 20 per cent to 100 per cent and beyond. The rise in agricultural labourers' wages was similarly put at 60 per cent over the period.

Turning to the question of whether there had been a corresponding increase or decrease in the price of goods and services over the same period, Giffen calculated that such prices were much the same in 1883 as they had been some fifty years earlier:

. . . There was a moderate rise of prices all round between the years 1847–50 . . . a rise not exceeding about 20% . . . yet within the last twenty years this rise has disappeared and prices are back to the level, or nearly to the level, of 1847–50. The conclusion is that, taking things in the mass, the sovereign goes as far as it did forty years ago. . . . If, in the interval, the average money earnings of the working classes have risen between 50% and 100%, there must have been an enormous change for the better in the means of the working man, unless by some wonderful accident it has happened that his special articles have changed in a different way from the general run of prices. (pp. 600–1)

Looking then at these 'special articles', Giffen found that, with few exceptions, the prices of products consumed by the working classes had in fact fallen over the fifty years in question. By far the most spectacular price fall had been for wheat, which throughout the period had remained the staple food of the poorer sectors of society: 'Take wheat. It is notorious that wheat, the staff of life, has been lower on the average of late years than it was before the free trade era. Even our fair trade friends, who find it so difficult to see very plain things, were forced to allow . . . that wheat is about 5s. a quarter cheaper on the average than it was' (p. 601). Giffen pointed out, however, that it was only in later years that the price of wheat had fallen significantly — while the average price of wheat in 1837–46 was 58s. 7d. it had been at 48s. 9d. only since 1873, a reduction not of 5s. but of 10s. This served to confirm that the repeal of the Corn Laws had not been followed by an immediate decline in average wheat prices and that prices had remained high until 1862 after which time they began to fall:

There is a still more important consideration. Averages are very good for certain purposes, but we all know in this place that a good deal sometimes turns upon the composition of the average, — upon whether it is made up of great extremes, or whether the individual elements depart very little from the average. This is specially important in a question of the price of food. The average of a necessary of life over a long period of years may be moderate, but if in some years the actual price is double what it is in other years, the fact of the average will in no way save from starvation at certain periods the workmen who may have a difficulty in making both ends meet in the best of times. What we find then is that fifty years ago the extremes were disastrous compared with what they are at the present time. In 1836 we find wheat touching 36s.: in 1838, 1939, 1840 and 1841, we find it touching 78s. 4d., 81s. 6d., 72s. 10d., and 76s. 1d.; in all cases double the price of the lowest year, and nearly double the 'average' of the decade; and in 1847 the price of 102s. 5d. or three times the price of the lowest period is touched. If we go back earlier we find still more startling extremes. We have such figures as 106s. 5d. in 1810; 126s. 6d. in 1812; 109s. 9d. in 1813, and 96s. 11d. in 1817; these figures being not merely the extremes touched, but the actual averages for the whole year . . . what we have to consider then is, that fifty years ago the working man with wages, on the average, about half, or not much more than half, what they are now, had at times to contend with a fluctuation in the price of bread which implied sheer starvation. Periodic starvation was, in fact, the condition of the masses of working men throughout the kingdom fifty years ago. . . . But within the last twenty years what do we find? Wheat has not been, on the average, for a whole year as high as 70s., the highest averages for any year being 64s. 5d. in 1867 and 63s. 9d. in 1868; while the highest average of the last ten years alone is 58s. 8d. in 1873; that is only about 10s. above the average of the whole period. In the twenty years, moreover, the highest price touched at any period was just over 70s., viz. 70s. 5d. in 1867 and 74s. 7d. in 1868; while in the last ten years the figure of 70s. was not even touched, the nearest approach to it being 68s. 9d. in 1877. Thus of late years there has been a steadily low price, which must have been an immense boon to the masses, and especially to the poorest. The rise of money wages has been such, I believe, that working men, for the most part, could have contended with extreme fluctuations in the price of bread better than they did fifty years ago. But they have not had the fluctuations to contend with. . . . Wheat had quite a special importance fifty years ago, and the fact that it no longer has the same importance — that we have ceased to think of it as people did fifty years ago — is itself significant. (pp. 601–3)

Having analysed the dramatic fall in wheat prices, Giffen then turned to the one food whose price had increased considerably over the same period — that of meat. Here, he was dismissive of any major impact on working-class living standards: 'The truth is, however, that meat fifty years ago was not an article of the workman's diet as it has since become. He had little more concern with its price than with the price of diamonds. The kind of meat which was mainly accessible to the workman fifty years ago, viz., bacon, has not, it will be seen, increased sensibly in price' (p. 603).

In Giffen's opinion, the increase in working-class wages, between the years 1830 and 1880, represented a real gain. Wages had increased while the prices of most necessary products had fallen, bringing about what he called a 'revolution' in their living conditions. At the same time, the people had benefited from increased government expenditure on public goods, better health care and improved sanitation. Pauperism had decreased

despite a constantly increasing population — those in receipt of
relief in England, Scotland and Ireland having fallen from
1,676,000 in 1849 to 1,014,000 in 1881. The number of depositors
at savings banks had risen from 429,000 in 1831 to 4,140,000 in
1881, with deposits increasing from £13,719,000 to £80,334,000
over the same period:

> We find undoubtedly that in longer life, in increased consumption of
> the chief commodities they use, in better education, in greater
> freedom from crime and pauperism, and in increased savings, the
> masses of the people are better, immensely better than they were
> fifty years ago. This is quite consistent with the fact, which we all
> lament, that there is a residuum still unimproved, but apparently a
> smaller residuum, both in proportion to the population and
> absolutely, than was the case fifty years ago; and with the fact that
> the improvement, measured even by a low ideal, is far too small. No
> one can contemplate the condition of the masses of the people
> without desiring something like a revolution for the better. Still, the
> fact of progress in the last fifty years — progress which is really
> enormous when a comparison is made with the former state of
> things — must be recognised. Discontent with the present must not
> make us forget that things have been so much worse. (pp. 611–12)

Pressing his case further, he concluded that the working classes
had not only seen their living standards dramatically improve,
but that virtually all of the country's great material improvements, in the period between 1830 and 1880, had gone to the
masses. The poor, he argued, were fewer, whilst those who
remained poor were individually twice as well off, on average,
as they had been. Based on available evidence, they had had, in
his opinion, almost all of the benefits which had accrued over
the period:

> The moral is a very obvious one. Whatever may be said as to the ideal
> perfection or imperfection of the present economic regime, the fact of
> so great an advance having been possible for the masses of the
> people in the last half-century is encouraging . . . (I am one of those
> who think that the regime is the best, the general result of a vast
> community living as the British nation does, with all the means of
> healthy life and civilization at command, being little short of a marvel
> if we only consider for a moment what vices of anarchy and misrule
> in society have had to be rooted out to make this marvel); still,
> whether best or not, it is something to know that vast improvement
> has been possible with this regime. Surely the lesson is that the
> nation ought to go on improving on the same lines. (p. 621)

Giffen ended with a strong endorsement of existing government policies and an appeal for free trade to continue as the
cornerstone of economic management. Not surprisingly, Gladstone, whose financial skills had long been admired by Giffen,
wrote that he had 'read with great pleasure your masterly paper
. . . and I hope it may be practicable to give it a wide circulation'.
However, the paper drew strong criticism from other quarters.
In a reply published in October 1884, Hutchinson, giving what
he termed 'a workman's view', said:

> Mr Giffen . . . has, with a pertinacity that would be amusing but for
> the damaging influence it is likely to have on the position and future
> prospects of the working man, promulgated, and repeated again and
> again, the statement that the working classes are now, and have
> been for some time, better off comparatively speaking than their
> employers; that they have been receiving the major portion of the
> profits of their labour; that they are less taxed in proportion to their
> means than any other class of society; and in addition to all this, they
> receive more benefits from the National Exchequer. Happy, happy,
> thrice happy working man! (p. 630)

Hutchinson did not dispute that the condition of the 'working
man' had indeed improved over the fifty years in question but
he took issue with Giffen as to the scale of these improvements.
He suspected, 'from oral information obtained in answers to
questions addressed to the older workmen in various trades',
that the increase in real money wages had been significantly
overstated in the 1883 paper, and he produced evidence from
the *Leeds Mercury* of 1835 to show that the prices of most
commodities (excluding flour) had, in fact, risen substantially by
1884. Most of all, he found Giffen's statement that meat had not
been a part of the working-class diet to be 'astounding' and
referred to Porter, who had claimed that over 50 per cent of the
poorest-paid class of labour had meat as a part of their regular
diet.

Looking at family budgets in the 1880s, Hutchinson went on
to discuss current living standards: 'Bread — the veritable staff
of life in a working man's home — is good and cheap, and
butcher's meat may, by waiting until Saturday night, be bought
for rather less money, so that the working man may have an
enjoyable dinner on Sunday; and, I say this advisedly, the

Sunday dinner is often, too often, the only meal, properly so called, that he and his family partake of during the week, the rest consisting of bread and meat, and tea, or coffee, or cocoa, a rasher of bacon, sausage, or any other shuffling excuse for a dinner that can be got for little money' (p. 634). Taking a 'sober and industrious' working person with three children and earning 20s. a week — a high estimate in Hutchinson's view — the family budget left only 2s. for clothing, education, and making provision for sickness, or any other unforeseen contingency. As the sum of two shillings was totally inadequate to meet these separate needs, Hutchinson argued, the only means of achieving them was self-denial, something which vast numbers of working men and women were in fact doing for the sake of their children: 'The working man is left now, practically, where he was in the days of Adam Smith — he is just about able to live by his labour and that is all' (p. 635).

Hutchinson was not alone in attacking the 1883 paper. Giffen's conclusions were held by many others to be far too optimistic, particularly by those who were pressing for sweeping social and economic reforms in the belief that industrial progress had tended to make the rich richer and the poor poorer. He was eventually obliged to respond to the many critics who had found his conclusions to be mistaken and unacceptable. He argued again (1885a) that general living standards had indeed improved beyond recognition and restated his belief that, on the basis of all available evidence: 'We may thus conclude that the vast increase of wealth and resources, which has undoubtedly taken place in the last century, has not been an increase for the benefit of a few, but that all classes have participated, and not least the artisan and labouring classes, the masses of the community' (p. 115). Again, notwithstanding the fact that there was still too much poverty: 'Even the very poor, however, are undoubtedly better off than the very poor of former times; and it may be doubted if they are more numerous than they were a century ago, when half the people of the United Kingdom were in that category' (p. 117).

That same year, writing in the *Contemporary Review*, Giffen (1885b) argued that the general increase in prosperity was such that it was, to a large extent, nullifying the effects of spasmodic downturns in trade:

Nothing can mark more forcibly the progress of modern communities than the outcry about depression which arises when the slightest decline from a maximum period occurs. The variations which were formerly from abundance to famine, affecting almost the entire community, are now limited to a small percentage of the total population, so that prosperity and adversity, according to the statistical evidence, are hardly distinguishable, and good business authorities maintain that the times when people complain most are the times that are really the best. (p. 802)

In 1886 Giffen gave a detailed reply to his detractors by presenting a further paper to the Statistical Society on the progress of the working classes. In this he set out to answer the specific criticisms made of the earlier paper and to look again at his overall conclusions. The 1883 paper had been attacked on the grounds that Giffen had been highly 'selective' in choosing a fifty-year comparison of living standards:

It has even been hinted, I believe, that being no friend of the working classes, and holding a brief from the capitalist classes, so called, against them, I selected the date of half a century ago with malice aforethought, knowing that the working classes were then in a state of special degradation; so that what I show as an improvement in their condition is really no more, or little more than a recovery of the position which they formerly held. (p. 29)

Not so, argued Giffen. Fifty years had been chosen because it happened to be the jubilee of the Statistical Society and also because it marked the beginning of various official statistical records which were indispensable to a study of the type he was undertaking. To those who would have preferred a shorter period of comparison, he argued that this would have intro- duced the danger of confusing business and trade cycles with long-term changes in living standards: '. . . if short periods only are taken into account, what is in fact an eddy in the main stream of events may be mistaken for the main stream itself. . . . A comparison for a period of fifty years in an age of great improvement is free from many of the difficulties incidental to a shorter period' (p. 30).

Giffen answered other critics who, in contrast, thought the fifty-year comparison too short by arguing that publica- tion of Porter's *Progress of the Nation*, in 1836, had shown that considerable gains had been made by the masses between 1800 and that date (a debatable point in the eyes of many), and he had therefore seen no reason to extend his own study back over a well-researched period. Secondly, prior to the 1830s, the country had been predominantly agricultural and any comparison with the heavily industrialised and urbanised 1880s would have been totally unjustified.

With regard to the argument surrounding the alleged rise in money wages, Giffen referred specifically to Hutchinson's criticism. The latter's 'oral information' that there had been no all round advance was dismissed as too subjective and with no statistical underpinning. In addition, Giffen claimed that when allowance was made for the fact that there had been a significant drift out of agricultural employment and into industrial occupations, and that working hours had been significantly reduced, the improvement in money wages had to be considered to be nearer 100 per cent than 50 per cent. With respect to changes in the composition of employment, he estimated that whilst roughly equal proportions were engaged in agricultural and non-agricultural work in the late 1830s, the division was 25 per cent and 75 per cent respectively in the 1880s. Allowing for the fact that industrial wages were substantially higher than those in the agricultural sector, the real advance must have been that much more substantial: 'What I have said may show that even an improvement of only 50% in wages, which nobody seems to question, comparing given employment with given employment, implies under the actual circumstances of a change in the composition of the working population, a much greater improvement on the average than 50%' (p. 38). Giffen also argued that the improvement in wages had been most marked amongst unskilled non-agricultural labour, estimating this improvement to have been between 70 per cent and 90 per cent. The greatest progress, therefore, had been made by those at the lowest end of the labour market, who represented by far the greatest proportion of the working population. It followed that, allowing also for the reduction in working hours which was not in dispute, the overall improvement was statistically very close to the 100 per cent quoted in the 1883 paper: 'Altogether, then, the incredulity with which the assertion of an average increase of 100% in the money wages of the working classes in the last fifty years, was received in some quarters, does not appear to have any justification' (p. 40).

Turning to the question of whether prices of basic foodstuffs and other necessary goods had risen or fallen in parallel with changes in money wages, Giffen once again referred to Hutchinson:

> On this head, I may remark, there is also practically no question raised, the only challenge I know of being that of Mr Hutchinson already referred to. Mr Hutchinson indeed gives a list of prices from the file of the 'Leeds Mercury' in 1835 and 1884, of a very curious description; but the list does not include clothing, while as to flour he admits himself that the average facts fifty years ago and at the present time do not correspond to the indication of the table. He might have said the same of potatoes and one or two other articles, including bacon, which has undoubtedly not risen in price on the average and comparing period with period, as he represents it. The facts remain undisputed that as regards breadstuffs, clothing, tropical produce, and miscellaneous articles of every sort, prices range lower at present than they did fifty years ago. *Per contra*, there has been an advance in meat, except bacon; but with this exception mainly, the change of prices in the last fifty years have benefited the workman. A sovereign goes farther than it did. (p. 47)

The extent of the improvement in the condition of the working class was emphasised by reference to the earlier writings of Carlyle, Disraeli and Gaskell. Carlyle speaking in *Sartor Resartus* of potatoes and point being the diet of the Irish peasant; Disraeli, in *Sybil*, describing the appalling squalor of the average working-class home and of labourers with as many as eight children surviving on 8s. a week; and Gaskell in *Mary Barton*, talking of families with no coal for the grate, no clothes for the bed and thin bones showing through ragged clothes.

Giffen also referred to a book, written some forty years previously, by Thornton (1846), and more specifically to the conditions of the Dorsetshire agricultural labourer who, with his wife and children, was subsisting on about 9s. per week and eating nothing but bread and potatoes, with an occasional slice of bacon. Similarly, the peasantry in Wiltshire and Somerset were seldom eating anything better than dry bread, whilst Welsh labourers lived on coarse barley bread, flummery and potatoes. Worst of all was Ulster, where the daily wage was about 1s., and in the south of Ireland it was as low as 8d. In the western parts of Ireland, the diet consisted only of potatoes bought out of a daily wage of 6d. Giffen also made use of Thornton's evidence of living conditions in the newly industrial-ised towns and cities — of nine thousand families in Manchester earning an average of 1s. per week; of over fifteen thousand people in Stockport whose weekly income was 1s. 4d., whilst the average weekly wage of the fully employed was 7s. 6d. and only 4s. 7d. for those who were in part-time employment.

Evidence such as this, Giffen argued, put the facts of the case beyond dispute, and the question as to whether living standards had substantially improved over the fifty years was no longer a matter for debate. One point, however, needed further clarifi-cation. Hutchinson had argued that Giffen's claim about meat not being a part of the working-class diet was incorrect and that this could be demonstrated by reference to statistics on the family diets of agricultural workers, collected by Porter in 1836. Giffen strongly attacked this claim:

> It is only too plain that the masses of Irish peasants and of English and Scotch agricultural labourers, as well as labourers in towns, who constituted a far larger proportion of the population of the country than the same classes do now, had most of them hardly any meat, very many none at all, in their diet, while the 'occasional' meat some of them had was seldom anything less than bacon. (pp. 55–6)

However, the Porter 'evidence' had still to be explained. Giffen found that it was contained in a summary of answers as to how the average labourer lived — answers received from enquiries made county by county throughout England. Upon closer examination of the individual county returns, however:

> . . . in only one of all the answers is meat *co nomine* spoken of; in all the others, where any sort of meat is spoken of, the word is bacon or pig-meat. Usually too the bacon is spoken of as only occasional. . . . We may thus see what the phrase 'with meat' means. It is an occasional bit of bacon only: this is what Mr Hutchinson means by meat forming a regular portion of the diet of the poorest paid class of labour fifty years ago. (p. 61)

Giffen's 1886 paper to the Statistical Society therefore strongly defended what he had said some three years earlier. On no

count did he feel that his arguments had been seriously
challenged — indeed, he restated his case with even greater
conviction:

> The general conclusion from all the facts is, that what has happened
> to the working classes in the last fifty years is not so much what may
> properly be called an improvement, as a revolution of the most
> remarkable description. The new possibilities implied in changes
> which in fifty years have substituted for millions of people in the
> United Kingdom who were constantly on the brink of starvation, and
> who suffered untold privations, new millions of artisans and fairly
> well-paid labourers, ought indeed to excite the hopes of philanthro-
> pists and public men. (p. 72)

For the future, Giffen argued, far greater advances were
possible if working men were thrifty and invested time and
effort in education. And here he allowed himself a rare personal
statement, tinged with pride in being a Scot:

> I am not speaking now theoretically; I know from experience, and
> from intimate acquaintance with working men themselves, using the
> words 'working men' this time in a popular sense, what can be done
> on very small means. It will be a shame to English working men if
> they cannot with comparatively ample means raise themselves to the
> standard of education which Scotch peasants have long since been
> able to reach with what, until recent years, were very narrow means.
> (p. 72)

In the discussion which followed presentation of Giffen's
paper to the Statistical Society, it was soon made apparent that
his view of working-class living standards in the 1880s was still
felt by many to be over-optimistic. Whilst the claim that the vast
majority of people had seen a much-needed improvement in
their conditions went unchallenged, it was felt that, given the
increased commitments of the urban worker — the need to
travel to and from work, payments for family education and for
sickness benefits — Giffen had been painting too rosy a picture
of present-day circumstances. In addition, although men were
paid higher wages, this increase was in many cases held to be
purely nominal, large numbers being out of work or working
part time. The theoretical rate of pay was kept up by the trade
unions and those who were out of work were, to a certain

extent, supported by those who were in work. Current wage rates were therefore not acceptable as a fair representation of the real earnings of the people.

It was also argued that, for London in particular, a great deal of the advance claimed by Giffen had 'ended in smoke'. The rents of working-class housing in the capital and in many other manufacturing centres had doubled over the fifty-year period. Furthermore, the increase in London wages had been nothing like as great as in the cases quoted by Giffen. Looking at all the facts, it was impossible to come to the conclusion that the working classes were twice as well off: that they were better off was beyond doubt, but by no more than 20 to 25 per cent.

Perhaps the greatest reservations concerning the Giffen papers of 1883 and 1886 related to the so-called 'residuum' — those people living on or near the breadline who had seen little or no material improvement in their living standards over the fifty years in question. A leader in *The Times* of 20 January 1886, whilst supporting Giffen's claim of a substantial improvement in general conditions, expressed concern on this point:

> There is, in the first place, nothing in Mr Giffen's figures to show that the conditions of the lowest and poorest classes of the community had not sunk still lower, while the average condition of the working classes in general has enormously improved. . . . The general standard of comfort may have been raised, but the number of those who fail to attain it may have increased at the same time, or at any rate, the interval which separates them from it may have widened. It is certain, that crime and pauperism have decreased, but it is not so certain that the condition of those classes which perpetually hover on the edge of pauperism and crime has improved.

Giffen was unrepentant. In 1887(a) he was invited to contribute to a book being edited by Thomas Ward on the *Reign of Queen Victoria*, and he reaffirmed his view:

> The fact of a great rise in the scale of living among all classes began to attract attention twenty years ago, and is in truth one of the notorious features of the economic history of the time. That a different impression has got about lately in some quarters appears to be due to an exaggerated impression of the relative mass of the residuum, which is not surprising when those who receive and diffuse such impressions neglect to make use of the statistical method in dealing with facts where statistics are absolutely necessary.

In a great community like that of England, even facts that are small relatively are likely to be large absolutely. It may well be, therefore, that there is a large residuum, and yet all the facts as to the masses generally, as here set forth, and which must be true, or no such progress of the nation in wealth could have taken place as what has in fact occurred, may also be true. There is no inconsistency between the two sets of facts. Only the residuum, though a big fact absolutely, is not really so very large when the great mass of the community is considered. The hope of dealing with it successfully, it may be added — though this is going a little out of my way — lies really in the fact that it is smaller relatively than it was, and that the nation is strong enough to feel its existence an opprobrium and a shame, and to grapple with it in a way that has never been grappled with before. How far the hope is well founded may be a question, for moral evils are peculiarly inveterate, but the nation is certainly not staggering under the nightmare of its residuum as it was staggering under the load of pauperism and connected evils fifty years ago. The evil is still great but it is in every way more manageable. (pp. 30–1)

In the same year, Giffen (1887b) gave an address in Manchester as President of the Economic Section of the British Association. For the first time, he felt obliged to qualify some of the optimism he had shown with respect to the country's material advance. Many critics, and especially those campaigning for a more protectionist trade policy were now arguing that, whilst there was no doubting the general improvement in living conditions since 1845, the rate of progress in the more recent years had been non-existent and the country had, in fact, been going backwards instead of advancing as it had done in the twenty to thirty years before 1875. Giffen was prepared to concede a part of this claim, believing it to be, 'tolerably safe to draw the conclusion that there has probably been a falling-off in the rate of material increase generally'. Nevertheless, he was at pains to point out that it was only the rate of increase which had fallen and that there was no question of either economic stagnation or reversal between 1875 and 1885. He also produced figures to show that paupers continued to represent a smaller proportion of the population over the period, from 4.2 per cent in 1870–4 down to 3 per cent in 1880–4. Again, he ended on a positive note: 'I see no cause to doubt that the future will be even more prosperous than in the past. The national life seems as fresh and vigorous as ever. The unrest and complaints of the last few years are not bad signs' (p. 647).

The *Spectator* was impressed by Giffen's balanced view, and
an editorial in September 1887 commented:

> Mr Giffen is essentially an unpopular economist. He wants the
> quality which, more than any other, enables a writer on his special
> subjects to catch the public ear. That quality is a taste for extreme
> statements — and a disposition to add ciphers to his figures. . . .
> Economists of this type may be optimists or pessimists, buoyed up
> by constantly renewed hope or desolated by continuous despair. The
> only feature they have in common is contempt, their clouds have no
> break. England is either marching on like John Brown's soul, to fresh
> triumphs over bad seasons, foreign rivalry, and a population
> continually growing in face of continually decreasing means of
> support; or she has spent her last shot, and she has nothing left to do
> save to compose her limbs in decent expectation of the inevitable
> end. It is the books and articles that embody one or other of these
> alternatives that find readers and make conversation; and to both
> alike, everything that Mr Giffen writes comes as a douche of cold
> water. There is always the same discouraging appeal to facts, the
> same call to verify conclusions, the same ruthless determination to
> include everything in the calculation, to pass by nothing that can
> affect the ultimate result.

Late the following year, Giffen (1888) read a further paper
before the now Royal Statistical Society in which he reaffirmed
his belief that the working population as a whole had indeed
continued to prosper since 1875 and offered a reason why the
advance had gone unrecognised by the protectionists. The
improvement was real he argued, but had been brought about
in a different way, for while the increase in wealth prior to 1873
had been due to a great rise in money incomes, accompanied by
a much smaller rise in commodity prices, after that date the
benefits had been received in the form of stationary or even
slightly declining incomes, accompanied by a great fall in prices.
Admittedly the rate of progress had been slower in the latter
period but had been far more substantial than was believed by
those who sought to gauge improvements only by reference to
changes in income. Giffen had made the same point in his
evidence to the Select Committee on Corn Averages in July 1888:
'It is quite obvious that you cannot go into the question of the
condition of the working classes by merely studying the money
wages; you have to study what the wages will buy; and it is very
convenient to have a public official record of the average prices

of important articles of working-class consumption. It might be desirable if those records could be somewhat extended.'

The debate over whether the working classes were in fact enjoying substantially better living conditions did not die down, and in 1889 Giffen was to return yet again to the controversies he himself had started with publication, in 1883, of his first paper on the subject. In an article for the *Contemporary Review*, he replied to those critics who had complained that improvements in money incomes had to be offset against several other factors — first, that there had been substantial increases in rents and in travel cost, second, that conditions of work had deteriorated and that the working population had to put more effort into earning their pay, and finally, that city life required people to spend far more on food, clothing and shelter than had hitherto been the case.

Here again, Giffen was to make some concession. With regard to rents, he admitted that, for those 'peasants' who had moved to the industrial areas away from the country villages where there was no monopoly rent, and who were now living 'in the slums of a great city, earning perhaps 15s. a week, but disbursing 4s. or 5s. for rent', there had been no real improvement in living standards: 'Comparing all the conditions, it may certainly be doubted whether the peasant . . . in exchanging the hard life of the country, which still had the advantage of being out in the open, for the hard life of the city, had made any real advance' (p. 833). However, in those cases where the peasant had achieved the status of town artisan, for whom money wages had shown such a marked advance, then the improvement in standards, monopoly rents notwithstanding, had been enormous.

For the first time, Giffen was also prepared to admit that the improvement in living standards had not been shared by the very poor. On average, he argued, there had been an enormous gain, but for the residuum nothing had changed, and his former insistence that this residuum was a relatively small 'problem' became more cautious:

Nothing can appear so deplorable or so hopeless as the conditions of the floating mass of rude labour in large cities. Monopoly rents in this case appear to sweep away all possible advantage which may result from higher money wage, comparing the labourer of the town with the labourer of the country. In many cases, even, it must be admitted, the 'residuary' of the city is on a lower level than the 'residuary' of the country. His 'net' earnings are less. . . . The absolute magnitude of the city residuum must not blind us to the fact that it may be, not an increasing, but a diminishing, element with reference to the population generally. . . . The assumption so often made, that the residuum is increasing relatively, is one which requires proof, and I have never seen any attempt at proof, while there are some broad facts, such as the diminution of serious crime and of pauperism, against it. (p. 834)

In 1889 Giffen had estimated that a family income of 15s., or less, per week had to be considered a residuum wage. In his evidence to the Labour Commission, which sat from 1892 to 1894, he had revised this estimate to include families whose total weekly earnings were 20s. per week, or less. Reporting to the Commission in January 1893, he also produced his calculations as to the actual earnings of adult males engaged in manual labour. These figures showed that nearly 24 per cent of men in employment were receiving wages of 20s. or less, which suggested that the residuum so often dismissed by Giffen as 'negligible' did in fact comprise nearly one quarter of all manual workers.

Giffen was aware of the glaring inconsistency between this statistic and his earlier dismissal of the residuum as a serious social and economic problem. His report was soon qualified. The 23.6 per cent, he argued, had to be seen in its proper context. First, there were a large number of agricultural workers included in the numbers, especially as the estimate related to Ireland as well as to Great Britain. Second, the figure was inflated by the fact that it included many skilled workers in the textile trades who were poorly paid but whose wives and children also tended to work in the mills, thus significantly increasing family incomes to well above 20s. per week. Finally, allowance had to be made for the fact that many of the men earning less than £1 were old and 'past the vigour of life'; whilst these men were still in employment, their average wages were well below the average for their respective trades.

After deducting agricultural and textile workers, and old men on half-pay, Giffen conceded that the greater part of residue did then appear to consist of less-skilled or casual workers, who

were to be found in the great cities, and particularly in London.
The Labour Commission concluded:

> This part of the population is to be found in great numbers in the
> East of London, where, according to the estimate made by Mr
> Charles Booth, in the result of his careful inquiries, about 22½ % of
> the total population (all ages and sexes) of the district with which he
> deals, or about 204,000 persons, belong to families in receipt of
> incomes of no more, on the average, than from 18s. to 21s. a week,
> while 11¼ % or about 100,000 of the same population, fall below this
> level, not including about 11,000 who belong to the lowest class of
> all. (Fifth and Final Report 1894, p. 11)

Giffen's earlier claim that the residuum 'though a big fact
absolutely is not really so very large when the great mass of the
community is considered' was now somewhat discredited and
the Reports of the Labour Commission must have made him
acutely uncomfortable in this particular respect. It was also
ironic that the evidence which established the real size of the
residuum was supplied by Giffen himself as the Board of Trade
witness to the Commission. Whilst he was prepared to concede
that the Commission's findings had established that the size of
the residuum was unacceptably high, he remained insistent,
however, that it was relatively smaller than in earlier years.

There can be no doubt that Booth's evidence on the London
poor was cause for further embarrassment, for his research
showed that the inner city residuum was far more substantial
than Giffen had assumed. At the same time, he was not at all
sympathetic to the methods adopted by social researchers,
however well intentioned their work might be, and he said so
openly in 1895:

> The obvious suggestion coming from a certain class of talkers about
> social phenomena, Socialists or semi-Socialists, and the miscellaneous
> philanthropists who think they can rush the reform of society and
> cure industrial malaise at a leap, is the rapid growth of a class within,
> but not of the general community, who are always out of employ-
> ment or have only casual employment, the classes forming the
> bottom groups of Mr Booth's well-known classification of the
> London population. The general idea of these talkers appears to be
> that the 'residuum' in our midst is enormously increasing, notwith-
> standing the general increase of wealth and rise of wages, and all the

other signs of increasing well-being . . . among the community as a whole.

All that need be said of this amiable talk is that it is absolutely without evidence and that it cannot be true. If the residuum were increasing rapidly, pauperism and crime would also be increasing. These are the outcome of a residuum and were abundant enough in former times when what would now be called the residuum constituted a large portion of the whole community. The idea has its origin in the recent study of social phenomena by well-meaning ladies and gentlemen who do not look at things in proportion, who are struck by the magnitude of the residuum they come in contact with, and who cannot realise, even if they stop to think at all, the conditions of a former society. (pp. 8–9)

In the same year, Giffen was responsible for publication of a *Board of Trade Blue Book* on manual labour and its earnings. Whilst the book was recognised as a skilful and elaborate computation of the earnings of the labouring population in the United Kingdom, Giffen specifically omitted any estimate of the number of men earning under £1 per week, even though this calculation had clearly been made. An editorial in the *Spectator*, however, focused on this omission:

Let us look a little closer at Sir Robert Giffen's figures. Though 24*s*. 7*d*. a week is the average wage per man, 24 per cent of the labouring classes have earnings below £1 a week. But for a man with a family to have less than £1 a week means that he is hardly within the region of civilisation. The Bishop who said that it was impossible to be a Christian on less than £1 a week, spoke, we fear, what was something very like the truth. Of course, there are exceptional cases; but, as a rule, less than £1 a week will not give men the chance to hire house-room and provide food and clothes for themselves and their families of the kind which conforms to a civilised standard, much less to purchase an occasional period of holiday leisure, to provide moderate recreations, to insure against sickness, and to obtain some reasonable facilities for self-improvement and cultivation. In a family in a town which is being brought up on less than £1 a week, there is not enough to spare for a halfpenny daily paper, for a treat to the children and the 'missis', or for any sort of amusement, unless the amount spent on house-hire is cut down to a point which makes the home unbearably squalid. Given the prices and habits of life that prevail in the United Kingdom, it is impossible to feel satisfied as long as there is any large percentage of the town population living below the £1-a-week level. The actual number of men computed by Sir Robert Giffen to be earning under £1 a week is not given in the Blue Book; but we presume that, taking the United Kingdom as a whole, there cannot be less than two million men in this position, and that most of these men are married, and have to support not merely themselves, but a wife and family. (28 September 1895)

In contrast to *The Times* which had welcomed the *Blue Book* as evidence of the significant advances made by the skilled and semi-skilled working class over the period 1886–92, the *Spectator* was once again revealing Giffen's tendency to be complacent about the plight of a residuum whose size he had clearly understated over many years. There is, however, every reason to suspect that Giffen, whose position at the Board of Trade gave him access to all significant statistical data relating to incomes and to living standards, played down the residuum issue, more by design than by accident, and that his motives were once again political.

On the subject of free trade, Robert Giffen had never been neutral. Some sixteen years earlier, in 1879, he had delivered his tract against the protectionists, arguing fiercely that prices could only be held down through free-trade policies and that cheap food was essential to future growth and prosperity. By 1895 the division between free traders and fair traders (i.e. protectionists) was as sharp as ever and the thrust of the protectionists' argument was directed at the need to create and protect jobs by moving to a policy of import restriction. It had never been in Giffen's interest, therefore, to acknowledge the continued existence of a large pool of casual and unemployed workers who had not benefited to some extent from the free-trade policies which had dominated the second half of the nineteenth century. On the contrary, it was necessary for him to stress the great material advances which had certainly been made by the population as a whole and to argue that, whilst a 'residuum' did remain, it was a diminishing rather than an increasing problem.

Giffen's concern that protectionist policies should not prevail was evident at all times. As a member of the Royal Commission on Agriculture, which sat from 1893 to 1897, he was himself called to give evidence to the Commission. Asked to interpret the statistical data he had presented, he lost no opportunity to argue against fair-trade solutions to the current agricultural depression; similarly, in cross-examining other witnesses to the Commission, his questions were always designed to prompt support for free trade rather than protectionist measures. Giffen had, in fact, seen the setting-up of the Commission as a major concession to agricultural landowners who were intent on making a case to justify the reimposition of duties on wheat and other imported raw materials. Fearful of a return to the days of the Corn Laws, he was clearly determined to destroy any arguments which would have strengthened the hand of the protectionists.

Giffen was determined not only to stop the landowners from regaining their former wealth and pre-eminence at the price of cheap food but also to meet attacks from another quarter. Protectionism had been taken up not only by the agricultural interests but also by political activists — the socialists — who saw import control as a means of securing better living conditions for a working class which was becoming more and more organised. What he saw as support for revolutionary rather than evolutionary social change was unacceptable to Giffen, the more so as free trade would be one of the first casualties of this new political philosophy. Again, the existence of a large residuum could only play into the hands of those seeking a more 'managed' economy, and Giffen quickly realised that *laissez-faire* supporters had, at the very least, to show that the benefits of open trade were, however slowly, being felt by increasing numbers of people at the lowest levels of society. The degree to which he felt vulnerable to the new socialist movement, however, is evident in his attacks on 'social researchers' (including Charles Booth) and on other 'well-meaning ladies and gentlemen' who were at pains to document the level and depth of inner-city deprivation.

Giffen's campaign for free trade continued throughout the 1890s. In a speech delivered at the annual dinner of the North Staffordshire Chamber of Commerce, in 1897, he extolled the virtues of the existing system and warned against the business community pressing for change: 'Business men, however, are sometimes found to rely on some hoped-for Protection from Government, and in this way I hope it will do some good, especially to the younger generation, if it is made clear, and yet again clear, that the time is past for Protection, and that no industry can live anywhere which is not able to face the most unrestricted competition' (p. 188). Writing in the *Economic*

Journal the following year, he again argued that the case for protectionism, far from being strong, had been totally discredited
by the available evidence and that the Fair Trade movement
must inevitably fail: 'Protectionist policy is thus opposed by the
force of circumstances, and another generation or two will
probably see the last Protectionist politician, not only in
England, but throughout the world. The breed, I am confident,
is very nearly extinct, because the modern atmosphere and
conditions, not theory, are making the policy next to impossible'
(p. 16).

Giffen's preoccupation with protectionism was to continue
through the turn of the century. His article, 'Financial retrospect,
1861–1901', published in 1902, restated the past gains made
under free trade; and in 1904 he argued that the future
prospects looked bright if protectionism could be kept at bay. At
the same time, his attitudes to diet and to the plight of the poor
were undergoing substantial change. In 1899, reviewing a
recently published essay on 'The wheat problem', Giffen
attacked the assumption that wheat still retained its traditional
position as the essential, staple food:

> Nowhere, according to Sir William Crookes' own showing, is so
> much wheat consumed per head as in France, the United Kingdom
> and the United States, the very countries in which its relative
> importance is lowest as an article of diet. . . .
> . . . Everyone knows, again, that flour itself in domestic economy
> is more and more being applied as an element in cooking articles of
> luxury, and that it is not being used to a large extent as a principal
> food at all. (pp. 170–1)

Such sentiments stood in marked contrast to those of the
1880s when Giffen's belief in bread as the staff of life could not
have been more strongly expressed. By 1900 he had clearly been
persuaded that the conditions which could give rise to the
'paradox' had largely disappeared, in so far as the great majority
of the population was concerned. He was also losing sympathy
with those who, according to other social observers, were still
living in extremes of poverty. Indeed, his views on the condition
of the poor were becoming increasingly reactionary and un-
sympathetic. Speaking to the British Association in 1903, he
argued:

. . . the question will arise, having regard to recent discussions, whether, in spite of the magnitude of the expenditure generally, there are not large numbers of the people insufficiently fed. The recent investigations of Mr Rowntree and Mr Booth would seem to point to a conclusion of this sort, though, for one, I must confess myself unconvinced. The dietary of prisons and workhouses, which is found quite sufficient for health, and, with not great additions, would be found quite sufficient for full work, is not so very expensive. The question is more a medical one than one to be settled in any way by statistics or general comparisons. There is no doubt that the waste in certain directions, if it could be repaired — I refer especially to the drink expenditure — would go far to provide the expenditure on food required for the proper nourishment of some of the children and families who are now insufficiently fed. (p. 587)

and referring in the same speech to the need for educational improvement, he attacked the laziness to be found in the working class:

One fault of the present time is that people have been taking things too easily. Our populations . . . have, to some extent, begun to play too soon, and they are not playing in the right way. They are giving to football and cricketing some of the time that should be given to severer employments, among which educational improvement comes first, and the additional labour necessary to find the means for that improvement. The next generation, it may be hoped, will be more laborious, more energetic, more studious and less athletic than the present. (p. 592)

The move to the right, both in economic and social terms, which characterised Giffen's later work cannot be considered exceptional for, by this time, a clear generation gap had developed between him and the younger more radical writers of the day who were acutely aware of Edwardian poverty and of the increasing problems associated with free trade. Quite simply, Giffen grew conservative with age — a phenomenon so commonplace that it is widely regarded as a part of the human condition.

He nevertheless remained an influential figure in public life. His decision to vote Unionist in 1909 and to break a lifetime association with the Liberals — accusing them of adopting 'socialist' policies — generated considerable interest in the press and elsewhere. Only one 'liberal' principle now remained — his other lifetime belief in the efficiency and fairness of free trade —

but his move across to the Unionists, who were in favour of greater tariff protection, was to bring about his conversion to the fair-trade cause.

In January 1910, some three months before his death, Giffen abandoned the uncompromising commitment he had held throughout his life. In a letter to *The Times* he wrote:

> Mr Balfour has shown most conclusively that some of the points most strongly argued by Tariff Reformers are consistent with Free Trade ideas and practice — that import duties as such are not opposed to Free Trade, nor are they to be altogether rejected if they have incidentally a slightly protective effect provided they are better on the whole than the taxes they would replace, such as excessive income tax and death duties. Liberal Free Traders in their advocacy have forgotten what is due to good finance and other practical considerations, and have adopted strange arguments, such as the alleged inconsistency between taxes on food and Free Trade. In reality there is a great deal in common between the aims of Free Traders of the old school, of Adam Smith, and Peel and Gladstone — I would even add Cobden — and the aims of the more moderate Tariff Reformers. (17 January 1910)

The younger Giffen would never have moved so far towards fair trade. But by this time he was 73 years old, more conservative, and he must have recognised, however painfully, that Victorian Britain was now relegated to the history books and that the Edwardian era was itself coming to an end. Solutions to the economic and social problems of the day were seen to lie in directions other than free trade, and the living conditions of the population, as a whole, were undergoing radical change. All this cannot detract, however, from the fact that by the time of his death, in April 1910, Robert Giffen's views on trade, and on the causes and relief of poverty, had been a force in shaping British economic and social policy for over forty years.

References

Giffen, R. (1867a) 'The reduction of the national debt', reprinted in R. Giffen (1880) *Essays in Finance*, 1st Series, George Bell & Sons, pp. 259–79.

Giffen, R. (1867b) 'Financial questions for the reformed Parliament', *Fortnightly Review*, Vol. 8 (Old Series), pp. 711–25.

Giffen, R. (1879a) 'On the fall of prices of commodities in recent years', *Journal of the Statistical Society*, Vol. 42 (March), pp. 36–68; with Discussion, pp. 69–78.

Giffen, R. (1879b) 'The new protection cry'. Written under the pseudonym 'Economist'.

Giffen, R. (1883) 'The progress of the working classes in the last half century', *Journal of the Statistical Society*, Vol. 46, pp. 593–622.

Giffen, R. (1885a) 'Some general uses of statistical knowledge', *Journal of the Statistical Society*, Jubilee Volume, pp. 96–127.

Giffen, R. (1885b) 'Trade depression and low prices', *Contemporary Review*, Vol. 47, pp. 800–22.

Giffen, R. (1886) 'Further notes on the progress of the working classes', *Journal of the Statistical Society*, Vol. 49 (March), pp. 28–91; with Discussion, pp. 92–100.

Giffen, R. (1887a) 'The growth and distribution of wealth', in T.H. Ward (ed.), *The Reign of Queen Victoria*, Vol. 2, Smith, Elder & Co., pp. 1–42.

Giffen, R. (1887b) 'The recent rate of material progress in England', *Journal of the Statistical Society*, Vol. 50, pp. 615–47.

Giffen, R. (1888) 'Recent changes in prices and incomes compared'. *Journal of the Royal Statistical Society*, Vol. 51, pp. 713–815.

Giffen, R. (1889) 'The gross and net gain of rising wages', *Contemporary Review*, Vol. 56, pp. 830–43.

Giffen, R. (1895) 'Depression corrected', *The Edinburgh Review*, Vol. 73 (July), pp. 1–26.

Giffen, R. (1897) 'Protectionist victories and free trade successes', published in *Economic Inquiries and Studies*, (1904), George Bell & Sons, pp. 178–88.

Giffen, R. (1898) 'Protection for manufacturers in new countries', *Economic Journal*, Vol. 8, pp. 3–16.

Giffen, R. (1899) 'The coming wheat scarcity', *Nature*, Vol. 61 (21 December), pp. 169–71.

Giffen, R. (1902) 'Financial retrospect, 1861–1901', *Journal of the Royal Statistical Society*, Vol. 65 (March), pp. 47–75.

Giffen, R. (1903) 'The wealth of the Empire and how it should be used', *Journal of the Royal Statistical Society*, Vol. 66 (October), pp. 582–98.

Giffen, R. (1904) 'The present economic conditions and outlook for the United Kingdom', in *Economic Inquiries and Studies*, pp. 405–30.

Hutchinson, J.G. (1884) 'Progress and wages', *Nineteenth Century*, Vol. 16, pp. 630–8.

Porter, G.R. (1836) *Progress of the Nation*, John Murray.

Thornton, W.T. (1846) *Over Population and Its Remedy*, Longmans, Brown, Green & Longmans.

CHAPTER 5

The Paradox Statement

Earlier chapters have focused on the life and career of Robert Giffen and on that part of his work most closely concerned with the conditions and progress of the poor in Victorian Britain. Having looked in some detail at the man and his writings, the controversy surrounding the origins of the paradox which first appeared in the third edition of Marshall's *Principles* can now be explored. Three questions remain unanswered. First, why should Marshall have felt it necessary to refer to the paradox at all in 1895? Second, how did Marshall come to know of Giffen's observation? Finally, when had Giffen himself observed the paradox? These three questions are now considered in greater detail.

The paradox reference in Book 3, Chapter 6 of the 1895 edition of Alfred Marshall's *Principles of Economics* was contained in a new section on the marginal utility of money which had been added to the third edition. The fact that Marshall felt the need to elaborate on this particular topic, and to make reference to Giffen's observation, is explained by events which followed publication of the second edition of *Principles* in 1891.

Writing on value and utility, Marshall had argued that although each purchase made by a person technically increases the marginal value of money to him by reducing his total purchasing power these changes in marginal utility were for the most part so small that they could be effectively ignored (in mathematical language, such elements were taken to belong to the second order of small quantities and were therefore insignificant).

In 1893 Professor J.S. Nicholson of Edinburgh University published his *Principles of Political Economy* and in an appendix to the third chapter he wrote a 'Note on Professor Marshall's

Treatment of Consumer's Rent' in which he took Marshall to
task for dismissing the effects of purchases on the marginal
utility of money. Referring to Marshall's *Principles* he observed:

> It is further assumed . . . that it is 'not necessary to take account for
> our present purpose of the possibility that the marginal utility of
> money to (a man) might be appreciably altered in the course of his
> purchases'. In the mathematical Note VI (p. 753) this assumption is
> stated still more explicitly, and made to rest on the ulterior assump-
> tion 'which underlies our whole reasoning, that the expenditure on
> any one thing, as for instance, coals, is only a small part of his whole
> expenditure'. . . . (pp. 63–4)
> . . . It is however clear that in all cases we must consider the
> marginal utility of money. . . . If we take the case of the ordinary
> consumer, the most obvious condition which he must always take
> account of is, that the more he spends the less he has to spend; and
> apart from this the great mass of the people spend the bulk of their
> earnings on a very few commodities. (p. 64)

Nicholson's reservations about Marshall's view of the marginal
utility of money drew a response from Professor Edgeworth.
Writing in the *Economic Journal* the following year, he challenged
Nicholson's claim that, so far as utility was concerned, 'we can
never get beyond one individual':

> Undoubtedly there is a great gulf between one's own and other
> people's feelings. But it must be leaped over by common sense, and
> bridged by sympathy. . . . Once it is admitted that other people's
> pleasures exist and may be reckoned like one's own, they come
> under the category of quantity, and are amenable, like other quan-
> tities, to the law of averages. . . . The cautious use of the principle of
> averages which Professor Marshall again and again insists on appears
> to me to fully meet the difficulty which Professor Nicholson finds in
> the diversity of individual dispositions. (p. 154)

Edgeworth's support of the Marshallian use of averages in developing a theory of utility and value failed to impress Nicholson
and he replied to Edgeworth in the following edition of the
Economic Journal. Referring again to the measurement of marginal
utility, he repeated his view that Marshall's approach could not
be justified:

> If with the same individual there are difficulties, if the shilling's
> worth of happiness from marginal purchases is as variable as the size

of the marginal parcels, the difficulties are increased with every individual we add to the number. Of course, if we assume that the individuals are similar and similarly situated — in mind, body and estate — we may add to their number indefinitely. But in this case the increase in numbers is purely formal. Professor Edgeworth attempts to get over the difficulty by reference to averages and to normal groups composed of normal proportions of rich, poor, sensitive and phlegmatic, but the similarity is only postulated and the conclusion is formal. . . . (p. 345)

. . . The point is that in considering expenditure 'we must always take into account the marginal utility of money', or less technically, we must consider that the utility of money increases with every portion spent, or in the vulgar, we cannot both eat our cake and have it. A theory of expenditure which neglects the two primary facts that incomes are limited, and that the utility of the money retained increases as it becomes smaller is in my view an unreal theory. It is only applicable to a few careless millionaires. (p. 346)

In a brief rejoinder to Nicholson in the same volume, Edgeworth did not retract his earlier opinions but took the controversy no further. However, discussion about the constancy of the marginal utility of money had clearly been a significant subject of debate in the years 1893 and 1894, and in the third edition of *Principles*, Marshall was obliged to make reference to the controversy and to defend his views. The support he had received from Edgeworth and others served to reassure him, and in a footnote to the third edition's section on consumer's surplus he commented: 'Professor Nicholson . . . , apparently under some misapprehension as to the drift of the doctrine of consumer's rent, has raised several objections to it, which have been answered by Professor Edgeworth . . .' (p. 203n). However, Nicholson had raised a very specific objection to Marshall's assumption that it was not necessary to take account of changes in a purchaser's command of money as a result of his making purchases. Whilst conceding that the marginal value of money does indeed change as spending increases, Marshall held these effects to be generally insignificant although, very exceptionally, they would have to be taken into consideration. This reply to Nicholson was then given in a new section which was included in the third edition and which gives us the Giffen paradox as the exceptional case:

The substance of our argument would not be affected if we took account of the fact that, the more a person spends on anything the less power he retains of purchasing more of it or of other things, and the greater is the value of money to him (in the technical language every fresh expenditure increases the marginal value of money to him). But though its substance would not be altered, its form would be made more intricate without any corresponding gain; for there are very few practical problems, in which the corrections to be made under this head would be of any importance.

There are however some exceptions. For instance, as Sir R. Giffen has pointed out. . . . (pp. 208–9)

Marshall, in short, remained convinced that, in the vast majority of cases, changes in the marginal utility of money brought about by additional spending (or by increases in the prices of necessaries) could be safely ignored. Giffen, however, had supplied a rare exception to the general rule and, to this limited extent, Nicholson had made his point.

* * *

Put in its proper context, the reason for Marshall's inclusion of the Giffen paradox in the third edition of *Principles* becomes clear — the statement contributed to a debate on value and utility which had been triggered by the publication of the first and second editions of *Principles* and which had involved Nicholson, Edgeworth and Marshall, three eminent professors of the day. However, a second problem remains — how did Marshall come to know of Giffen's paradox?

The mystery would have been solved long ago had Marshall referenced the observation attributed to Giffen. However, there is no information offered either with regard to the precise origins of the paradox or to Giffen's own reference to such perverse consumer behaviour. Furthermore, no 'clues' are given elsewhere in *Principles* which could help unravel the mystery. But Marshall had clearly read something which made reference to the paradox, for in his 1909 letter to Edgeworth he talked of 'seeing Giffen's hint on the subject' (Pigou 1925). However, research has failed to produce any reference to the paradox by Giffen in the period between publication of the second and third editions of *Principles*. Moreover, a wider, more comprehensive search of Giffen's books, articles and letters to the press, of his attributed work as a senior civil servant and of his reports and evidence to Select Committees and Royal Commissions (see Bibliographical Notes) also fails to produce any earlier statement of the paradox.

It is possible that Marshall was overgenerous in attributing the paradox observation to Giffen and that he himself had recognised evidence of such unusual behaviour in some statistical data compiled by Giffen. Indeed, Stigler claimed that Giffen lacked the subtlety to observe and recognise the paradox and that it is better referred to as 'Marshall's Paradox'. This claim lacks substance, however. Giffen was an astute statistician and economist, with a keen political sense, and his work bears witness to this fact. In no sense did he lack subtlety. Furthermore, his early life and the writings which show both concern for the material progress of the working classes and a fascination with paradoxes would have made him highly sensitive to such behaviour and to note and comment upon it.

The argument that Marshall saw the paradox in statistical form is given some added weight by the fact that he wrote of seeing Giffen's 'hint' on the subject. This suggests something less than a clear statement of the paradox. At the same time Giffen was known to be no admirer of family budget studies, and such material is not commonly seen in his statistical work. Disaggregated data was also something of a rarity throughout the nineteenth century as Giffen himself conceded.

Other possibilities need to be considered. It is, of course, possible that a written statement did (and does) exist but is not directly attributable to Giffen. Reference to the paradox could have appeared, for example, in anonymous journal articles. Giffen was a prolific author and certainly wrote anonymously on many occasions — a fact which he acknowledged in the Preface to his *Economic Inquiries and Studies*, published in 1904. Much unattributable work must also have been produced during his years spent as a journalist, up to 1876. And the paradox statement could also have appeared in unsigned papers submitted by Giffen to Royal Commissions or Select Committees in his capacity as a senior Board of Trade official — documents which must still lie among the vast civil service paperwork of the last century.

While a case can be made for the anonymous statement or statistic, it remains an improbable explanation. How would Alfred Marshall have come to know of such evidence, and know also that Giffen was the author? It is possible that Marshall was sufficiently aware of Giffen's writing 'style' to be able to recognise his work. Similarly, if he had seen the paradox in a Board of Trade document he could easily have assumed that Giffen was the writer or that he carried ultimate responsibility for the document's contents. However, Marshall's attribution to Giffen in the third edition of *Principles* is quite explicit — a fact which suggests something far more substantial than an educated guess. It would moreover have broken with the strong Victorian code in defence of anonymity for Marshall to have named Giffen without confirmation and permission. Without Giffen's consent, Marshall would have referred to the original source material but would not have named Giffen. And if Giffen had agreed to be identified as author, Marshall would have referred to the material and associated it explicitly with Giffen. In fact, the reference in *Principles* falls in neither category.

Marshall, however, had *seen* a Giffen reference to the paradox. If so, and he was able to name Giffen, why was he then not able to provide a more detailed reference? A further, and most likely, possibility exists — that Giffen had indeed observed and commented upon the paradox on one or more occasions, but that he had never made written reference to it before discussing such exceptional behaviour with Alfred Marshall in correspondence, between 1891 and 1895. It is certain that the two men were well acquainted after 1880. Both were members of the Royal Statistical Society and the Royal Economic Society and they served together on the Monetary Committee of the British Association for several years after 1887. They also met through their association with Royal Commissions and Select Committees (Marshall, in fact, cross-examined Giffen in great detail as a member of the 1892–4 Labour Commission). It is entirely possible, therefore, that the paradox was raised in correspondence, with Giffen recalling that he had once observed behaviour which ran counter to Marshall's universal law of demand and describing the circumstances under which such behaviour had occurred.

Marshall would have been alive to discussion of the paradox after 1891, as he would have been aware of the implications of such behaviour for the theories he was developing with regard to the marginal utility of money. The paradox, in effect, supported Nicholson's claim that income changes — brought about by purchases of necessaries (or equally by price increases of necessaries) — could not be ignored in so far as the very poor were concerned. Having learnt of the existence of such exceptional behaviour from Giffen (a man he much admired and respected) Marshall would then have felt obliged to concede the point to Nicholson in the third edition of *Principles,* stressing that it was the rare exception which proved the general rule of utility and value. In essence, Marshall could have felt compelled to sacrifice a pawn in order to protect his queen.

The interest which Marshall would have had in the paradox is immediately evident. But what would have prompted Giffen to refer to such behaviour? He may, of course, have become directly involved with the controversies surrounding marginal utility theory. It is interesting to note that Giffen shared membership of the Monetary Committee of the British Association (1887–90) not only with Marshall but also with Edgeworth and Nicholson. These men were members of the same clubs and would meet frequently in London and elsewhere to discuss matters of mutual interest. It is possible, therefore, that the paradox was raised in discussion as a special case, with regard to utility theory. Giffen was known throughout his life as a lover of paradoxes and would have relished the thought of having been able to puncture any carefully measured theory of economic behaviour.

Discussion of the paradox in the early 1890s would also have offered another major benefit to Giffen — and for reasons entirely unconnected with any theoretical debate among academics in progress at that time. From 1893 to 1897 he was a member of the Royal Commission on Agricultural Depression which had been set up to examine the performance of and prospects for the agricultural sector of the economy. A major item on the agenda was, inevitably, the case for and against the imposition of taxes on imported wheat, as a means of improving agricultural profitability and investment into the twentieth century.

Throughout the period that the Commission sat, the landed interest was bringing substantial pressure to bear on politicians for the reintroduction of import duties on wheat. No friend of the landowner, and anxious to avoid any return to what he saw as Corn Law conditions, Giffen's cross-examination of witnesses and his own evidence to the Commission was directed against the protectionists. Any reintroduction of import taxes, he argued, might well protect UK wheat growers but, at the same time, it would have disastrous effects on the consumption of other products (whether agricultural or industrial) and would be a recipe for recession. In particular, the poor, who in Giffen's view had improved their living standards so noticeably since the removal of import taxes on wheat, would once again find their discretionary income reduced to the point where purchases of non-necessaries were severely reduced: a change which would, in turn, have serious consequences for commerce and industry in general.

Given the nature of the paradox, Giffen would have had every incentive to 'broadcast' this observation of the effect of bread price rises on the poor as a part of his warning against returning to the hard times experienced by large sectors of the working class in the days when, lacking adequate compensatory imports of wheat, UK harvest failures served only to raise bread prices to levels which pushed millions of people below the poverty line. Reference to the paradox in the third edition of *Principles* in 1895 would have served not only to reinforce the argument but, with Marshall's authority behind it, would also have helped to enlist the support of other influential academics for the free-trade cause.

Overall, the balance of probability suggests that Marshall had his attention drawn to the paradox by Giffen between the publication of the second and third editions of *Principles*. We have no record of notes or letters exchanged on the subject by the two men but there is no doubt that they were writing to each other on both personal and academic issues throughout the 1890s and that their correspondence continued through into the twentieth century. There is some hope that letters relating to the paradox will yet come to light and it is to such evidence alone that we should look to explain Marshall's reference to the paradox in the 1895 edition of *Principles*. Equally, there is no reason to suppose that Marshall was ever directed by Giffen to any earlier, clear statement of the paradox or to statistical data prepared by Giffen which demonstrated paradox behaviour.

This lack of hard evidence would also explain, in large part, Marshall's later inability to defend the paradox when challenged to do so by Edgeworth. Marshall in fact believed that Giffen's paradox could occur but had been offered nothing of substance with which to demonstrate that it had.

* * *

A third and final question was posed at the beginning of this chapter, namely when had Giffen himself observed the paradox? Here we can be far more positive with regard to the time period involved.

First, and for a number of reasons, Giffen's observation of paradox behaviour was almost certainly made in the period before 1880. The paradox is concerned with the consumption of bread and with the effect on consumption of bread price rises. It relates, in particular, to those among the very poor for whom bread constituted a large part of the family expenditure on food and whose income was taken to be low and static. By 1880 the conditions under which the paradox could be widely observed were, certainly *in Giffen's view*, not at all common. Bread prices were falling on average, and the 1879 UK wheat harvest, though a failure, had brought about no increase in the price of bread. Indeed, prices continued to fall due to the effect of cheap imported wheat which was brought in to make up the deficiency in supply. At the same time incomes were rising for all classes, and dependence on the loaf to the extent implied by the paradox was becoming, *again in Giffen's eyes*, something of a rarity. This trend of falling bread prices and rising incomes was to continue for the rest of the century.

A further persuasive factor which helps to set an upper limit on the date of the original paradox observation comes in 1880 from the *Journal of the Statistical Society*. On 11 May of that year, two papers were read in London before the Society. The first, by Captain P.G. Craigie (Secretary of the Central Chamber of Agriculture) was entitled 'Ten years statistics of British agriculture 1870–1879' and was immediately followed by a second related paper presented by J.B. Lawes and J.H. Gilbert on 'The home produce, imports, consumption and price of wheat over twenty-eight (or twenty-seven) harvest years, 1852–53 to 1879–80 inclusive'. A discussion followed presentation of these two papers and the proceedings were subsequently reported in the June 1880 edition of the *Journal of the Statistical Society*, of which Robert Giffen was then editor.

In the journal's edited notes of the discussion, following presentation of the papers, the contribution of a Mr E. Power, a London corn merchant, is recorded. The report of Power's comments on the second paper read in part:

> The information had been on the whole relatively correct, and it had been a very good guide. In one part of the paper attention was called to the lower prices of wheat increasing consumption, but he was himself disposed to think that low priced bread tends rather to decrease than increase the consumption, because bread is always the cheapest food, and when the price of bread is high, the main bread-eating population are unable to get much meat, and are obliged to live more largely on bread. (p. 333)

This is a clear statement of the paradox. Furthermore, it is certain that Giffen himself was present during the discussion for he volunteered a point of information later in the evening with regard to the agricultural returns (p. 339). The statement by Power, therefore, was made not only in Giffen's presence but subsequently in the journal of which Giffen was editor.

Alfred Marshall had been elected a Fellow of the Statistical Society in January 1880 and would certainly have received and read the Society's journal which appeared in June of that year. Indeed, he may very well have been present on the evening in question, although there is no record of his having taken part in the discussion following presentation of the two papers. In any event, it is reasonable to suppose that he either heard or read Power's statement of the paradox. In his 'Memorandum on the fiscal policy of international trade', written in 1903, Marshall subsequently expressed his belief that Giffen seemed to have been the first to point out the paradox. This again would indicate that reference to the phenomenon by Giffen himself was made before 1880.

The probability that Giffen first observed and noted the paradox prior to 1880 is further strengthened by later references

made by both Marshall and Giffen. In his 1909 letter to Edgeworth (Pigou 1925), Marshall talked of the paradox occurring
'when wheat was dear and men were cheap' — a clear reference
to the period before 1880. And Giffen, commenting in the
Economic Journal's 'City Notes' in 1909 on recent rises in the
prices of wheat and meat, wrote: 'Fears are expressed that this
rise in wheat will affect the consumption of the working classes
seriously, and be bad for trade, but this is contrary to long
experience. Until thirty years ago, wheat was always thought
cheap when it was anywhere under 50s.' (p. 334).

There was, in fact, good reason for both Marshall and Giffen
to believe that 1879–80 was a watershed in terms of the general
living conditions of the poor. First, imports of cheap American
wheat had removed dependence on UK harvests to such an
extent that domestic crop failures after 1879 had only limited
effects on wheat prices and certainly were incapable of reversing
the long-term downward trend in prices which cheap imports
had allowed. Second, after 1880 the poor were able to bring a
greater variety into their diet and were certainly moving away
from the level of dependence on bread which is implied by the
Giffen paradox.

This of course is not to argue that the poor were now
prospering and lacked little in terms of food, clothing and
shelter. The most cursory examination of the social and
economic history of the times quickly establishes a degree of
deprivation and malnutrition which was unacceptable to many
Victorians. But paradox behaviour drives people to subsist on
little other than bread and to have no money available for
significant quantities of any other food. In Giffen's view, by 1880
such conditions were fast disappearing.

Giffen, however, was not complacent about the situation, and
thought that the progress which had been made by the end of
the 1870s was still fragile. In 1879, writing under the pseudonym
'Economist', he published a free-trade pamphlet in which he
attacked the arguments of the protectionists and in particular
the proposal that a substantial tax should be placed upon
imports of American corn. If such a tax were to be imposed, he
argued, then the days when wheat was dear and men were
cheap would quickly return, bringing with them the starvation

conditions which a large part of the population had known in earlier years. Cheaper bread was underpinning what progress had been made and any reverse would be disastrous:

> Now, bread and bread-stuffs stand in a particular position. Among the poor, no other articles of food can to any appreciable extent be substituted for it, and its consumption in the country generally cannot be substantially diminished unless the increase in price has the effect of causing a portion of the population to be under-fed or partially starved. I imagine that it is not the intention of any of those who proposed to change our fiscal system that one of the results should be the semi-starvation of a portion of the population. (p. 6)

By 1879, therefore, Giffen believed that the poverty which had produced the 'bread diet' of the paradox was being left behind and that only political and economic mismanagement could reverse this increasing material wellbeing.

The evidence for a pre-1880 Giffen paradox is therefore strong. But can we be equally confident about the date after which Giffen observed the phenomenon? Here, again, Marshall's 1895 reference and Giffen's own writings offer valuable clues.

The paradox, as described in Marshall's third edition of *Principles*, points to the poorer labouring classes giving up meat and the more expensive, farinaceous foods. According to his reply to criticism of his 1883 paper (on the progress of the working classes), Giffen believed that consumption of butcher's meat, prior to 1840, was virtually non-existent and that only after 1850 was meat eaten in any significant quantity by the poorer labourers. He was not alone in this view, for James Caird, the eminent statistician, had also argued (1868): 'When the policy of protection to agriculture finally disappeared in 1848 the great bulk of the people had ceased to know anything of butcher's meat, except as an occasional Sunday luxury' (p. 128). Similarly, the possibility that the residuum were eating 'more expensive farinaceous foods' prior to 1850 can be safely discounted, for it was only later that real incomes had improved sufficiently to allow the poor to purchase a limited amount of the luxury food products (cakes, biscuits, etc.) which before 1850 lay well beyond their means.

It can be argued that paradox conditions existed prior to the introduction of the Corn Laws in 1816, and that Giffen was in fact referring to this period when he identified the paradox. Certainly references made at that time (see Chapter 7) suggest that something close to paradox behaviour could be observed in England. However, Salaman (1949) has pointed out that after 1770, meat had all but vanished from the tables of the English poor as provisions began to get scarcer and dearer, and bread and cheese came to constitute the staple food of the masses. Given Marshall's reference to the poor sacrificing meat and the more expensive farinaceous foods, it is clear that, while demand for bread may well have risen when bread prices rose at the end of the eighteenth century and in the early years of the nineteenth century, this did not form the basis of Giffen's own evidence for the paradox.

* * *

Analysis of the paradox statement and of Giffen's own observations, with regard to the social and economic conditions of the Victorian working classes, suggests that Giffen first observed and noted the paradox between the years 1850–1880, at a time when the high price of wheat and the relatively low incomes of the labouring classes were creating an economic climate ideally suited to producing such exceptional consumer behaviour. This, of course, is not meant to argue that paradox behaviour could not be observed at all after 1880 when poverty and deprivation were certainly still very much in evidence. However, we are concerned here with *Giffen's* paradox, that is, with his own personal observation of the 'perverse' demand for bread brought about by conditions of extreme poverty. A broader view of the paradox will be taken in a later chapter. More immediately, however, the social and economic conditions of the United Kingdom between 1850 and 1880 need to be examined in greater detail to look for evidence of paradox behaviour which could have formed the basis of Giffen's observation.

References

Caird, J. (1868) 'On the agricultural statistics of the United Kingdom', *Journal of the Statistical Society*, Vol. 31 (June), pp. 127–45.

Craigie, P.G. (1880) 'Ten years statistics of British agriculture 1870–1879', *Journal of the Statistical Society*, Vol. 43 (June), pp. 275–312.

Edgeworth, F.Y. (1894) 'Professor J.S. Nicholson on "Consumer's Rent"', *Economic Journal*, Vol. 4 (March), pp. 151–8.

Giffen, R. (1879) 'The new protection cry'. Written as a political tract under the pseudonym 'Economist'.

Giffen, R. (1904) *Economic Inquiries and Studies*, George Bell & Sons. Esp. p. viii: 'I was writing anonymously as long ago as 1869'.

Giffen, R. (1909) 'City Notes', *Economic Journal*, Vol. 19 (June), pp. 332–5.

Lawes, J.B. and Gilbert, J.H. (1880) 'The home produce, imports, consumption and price of wheat over twenty-eight (or twenty-seven) harvest years, 1852–53 to 1879–80 inclusive', *Journal of the Statistical Society*, Vol. 43, June, pp. 313–31.

Marshall, A. (1895), *Principles of Economics*, (3rd edn), Macmillan.

Marshall, A. (1903) 'Memorandum on the fiscal policy of international trade', in J.M. Keynes (ed.) (1926) *Official Papers by Alfred Marshall*, Macmillan. Revised for publication in 1909.

Nicholson, J.S. (1893) *Principles of Political Economy*, Vol. 1, Adam & Charles Black.

Nicholson, J.S. (1894) 'The measurement of utility by money', *Economic Journal*, Vol. 4, June, pp. 342–7.

Pigou, A.C. (ed.) (1925) *Memorials of Alfred Marshall*, Macmillan, pp. 438–9.

Salaman, R.N. (1949) *The History and Social Influence of the Potato*, Cambridge University Press.

CHAPTER 6

Giffen's Paradox

The period between 1850 and 1880 produced social and economic conditions well suited to the paradox. But precisely where and when was such behaviour likely to have been observed by Giffen? In order to know more about place and time it is necessary to look first at the different regions of the United Kingdom and in particular at working-class regional diets over the thirty years in question.

Before undertaking any detailed regional analysis, however, the groups within which paradox behaviour could have occurred need to be identified. Marshall makes it clear that when Giffen referred to the paradox, he was talking about those whose basic staple food was bread and was not concerned with those for whom the potato was the mainstay of the diet. Marshall himself subsequently made no reference to potatoes when discussing the paradox, and such behaviour was clearly seen as a phenomenon to be found among those groups commonly referred to in Victorian Britain as the 'bread-eaters'.

This distinction between bread- and potato-eaters is central to research into the Giffen paradox. Many writers on the subject have looked for evidence of the paradox, not among bread-eaters but among those other groups whose staple food was the potato. The American economist, Paul Samuelson, wrote in 1964:

> When the 1845 Irish famine greatly raised the price of potatoes, families who consumed a lot of potatoes merely because they were too poor to consume much meat might have ended up consuming more rather than less of the high-price potatoes. Why? Because now they had to spend so much on potatoes, the necessary of life, as to make it quite impossible to afford any meat at all and hence were forced to become even more dependent than before on potatoes. . . .

> This curiosum is attributed to Sir Francis (sic) Giffen, a Victorian economist (p. 432).

This Irish 'fallacy' has been taken up by many others. However, attempts to explain the Giffen paradox in the context of the Irish potato famines of the 1840s not only lack empirical support, but, as Dwyer and Lindsay (1984) have shown, they are unrealistic. First, one cannot casually substitute potatoes for wheat in theories which refer specifically to the price and consumption of bread. Second, during the famines there were not more but fewer potatoes available and so the poor were simply unable to eat more, even had they wished to do so. Third, the poorest Irish families subsisted almost entirely on potatoes — meat consumption was unknown to the vast majority of mid-nineteenth-century Irish peasants — and the substitution of potatoes for 'luxuries' was out of the question. Finally, the mass of the Irish lived off the land — they did not purchase potatoes, in any modern sense, but ate what they grew — and the market sophistication implied in the Giffen paradox was absent.

It is therefore to bread-eaters that we must look for evidence of Giffen's own paradox. Having established this, a careful regional analysis of the United Kingdom between the years 1850 and 1880 allows us to narrow the area of search for such exceptional behaviour.

*　*　*

It is certain that Giffen's paradox did not relate to conditions in Ireland during the disastrous potato famines experienced in the 1840s. However, it is still important to extend the search beyond 1850 to establish whether the Irish economy changed quickly and substantially from its dependence on the potato after the famines and whether the population became a bread-eating rather than a potato-eating peasantry.

The search need not detain us for long. As Salaman (1949) has pointed out, the supremacy of the potato was scarcely shaken in Ireland for another thirty years after the famine. Diet changed slowly only after the passing of the 1870 Land Act, but in 1879 the peasantry and small farmers were still dependent on the potato to what was seen as a dangerous degree. Ireland had, in fact, developed a well-entrenched potato culture, evidenced by the fact that the Irish who emigrated to England throughout the 1840–70 period lived very much as they had done in their old homes — that is, almost exclusively on potatoes. This culture was to persist for another two generations.

Between 1850 and 1880, bread-eating on any significant scale existed only in Dublin. It is certainly true that the more affluent families in the capital placed bread well above potatoes in their staple food priorities and consumed significant amounts over the thirty years in question. However, though Dublin at the time was often more English than Irish, the number of bread-eating Anglo-Irish expressed as a proportion of the total population was insignificant. Considerable quantities of wheat were in fact produced in Ireland but the great majority was exported to England and Scotland (an export trade which continued even at the height of the 1840s potato famines, a fact still remembered by the Irish). Overall, Ireland was a potato-eating nation and this was not to change significantly until after the turn of the century. Giffen's paradox, equally, was no Irish phenomenon.

The potato culture of the Irish which persisted throughout the nineteenth century was also to be found in another part of the United Kingdom, namely the Highlands and Islands of Scotland. The Highlanders, close relatives of the Irish as Gaelic-speaking Celts, depended on this single crop to an equal extent. A Famine Relief Committee of 1846 found, for example, that on average potatoes constituted between three-quarters and seven-eighths of the food of Highland families, and the restrictive economic and social conditions of the clan system offered little or no incentive to broaden the diet. Barley was grown in some quantity but went almost exclusively to the whisky distilleries, which in most years pre-empted the entire barley crop. Potatoes had also largely succeeded in supplanting oatmeal through a combination of poverty and indolence. By the middle of the century, the broad mass of Highland people were living almost exclusively on the potato; coastal crofters could supplement this diet with fish, and those in the Hebrides who had salt to add to their potatoes were considered lucky.

The most varied diets were to be found not on the mainland

but in the Orkneys and Shetlands where the potato, though widely used, was never allowed to dominate the local economy to the same extent as in the Highlands. It was accepted as a useful food but the Islanders also had fish, oats and barley, and they looked to other vegetables such as broccoli, turnips, carrots and artichokes — crops which had never been seriously cultivated in the Highlands. Overall, the domination of the potato on the mainland was such that the Highlanders can be disregarded as wheat-eaters in the nineteenth century. Certainly, the Highlands did not provide conditions under which the paradox could be observed.

In sharp contrast to the agriculture and family diets of the Scottish Highlands, the Lowlands of Scotland enjoyed far more diverse and prosperous conditions throughout the nineteenth century. The potato was certainly grown in quantity but it was used only as an accessory food. Large amounts were cultivated to serve markets in Edinburgh, Glasgow and the industrial centres of the Clyde — cities which were predominantly bread-eating but which demanded the potato as a complement to meat. In addition, the Lowlands supplied potatoes to northern England and sent many thousands of tons a year to London. Seed potatoes, recognised for their particularly good quality, were also exported in quantity to England. However, in the Lowlands themselves, unlike the Highlands, the potato never dominated the urban or rural family diet.

The Lowlanders enjoyed a reasonably varied diet — bread and flour, barley, oatmeal and a wide range of root crops — which significantly increased the nutritional well-being of the poorer rural workers. Scottish Lowland husbandry had earned a reputation for high standards of cultivation and land management and working-class diets reflected this efficiency. With regard to bread-eating, by far the greatest consumption was to be found in Glasgow and Edinburgh where the relative affluence of industrial workers had stimulated demand for bread, meat and potatoes. Indeed, a large part of the agricultural land of the Lowlands was given over to growing the cereals and vegetables, and raising the cattle needed to supply the cities and larger towns with their food.

In geographic terms, Scotland cannot be regarded as a predominantly wheat-growing or bread-eating country in the middle Victorian years. The Highlands subsisted mainly on potatoes whilst large tracts of the Lowlands were given over to cattle and crops other than wheat. In fact, a large part of total grain requirements was imported either from England or from overseas. In demographic terms, however, a significant proportion of Scots were bread-eating, for the large cities were attracting an increasing number of people away from rural areas as industrial development generated more and more relatively well-paid jobs.

As for Wales, the country remained essentially an agricultural community of peasant proprietors carrying on, in the main, a system of subsistence farming throughout the second half of the nineteenth century. Small farmers and freeholders were everywhere and for those occupied in corn production (a crop not well suited to Welsh conditions) life was particularly precarious. By far the greater number, however, farmed in pasture districts and supplied the towns in their neighbourhood with milk and vegetables.

Unlike the Scottish Lowlands, Wales had shown itself unable to develop any large-scale arable farming which could supply the cereal crops demanded by the industrialising cities in the south of the country and, as bread was, without question, the basic staple food demanded in these new cities, much grain had to be imported from outside. Throughout the Victorian years there was a considerable influx of people to the industrial areas. The great wealth of coal in Wales, and the rapid development of manufacturing industry and the railways, created so great a demand for labour that money wages in the 1860s were often higher than those offered in England (Report of the Labour Commission, 1867). As in Scotland, bread-eating in Wales was concentrated in the new cities, although both rural and urban Welsh had always placed a high priority on bread as the foremost staple food. The potato culture of the Scottish Highlands would have been unacceptable to all but the poorest Welsh families.

Notwithstanding the substantial demand for bread, generated by the larger Celtic cities of the United Kingdom, the great Victorian bread-eaters were undoubtedly the English. England was a significant wheat-producing country which had, over the years, developed a clear and unambiguous 'bread culture'. No food took priority over bread, whatever its price, and severe shortages would produce riots and social unrest. The bulk of English wheat was grown along the eastern and southern seaboards, from Yorkshire to Devon, and the adjoining inland counties. In 1868 England supplied approximately nine-tenths of all domestically grown wheat, with Scotland and Ireland together contributing the remaining tenth. After the repeal of the Corn Laws, substantial imports were made to supplement English production, particularly in those years when the home harvest failed.

English demand for bread came from rural and industrial workers alike. Early-nineteenth-century attempts to introduce the potato as the primary staple food were abandoned when it became clear that the initiative had clearly failed. Potatoes were accepted by the English only as an accessory food — to accompany meat where possible — but they never made real inroads into the demand for bread. Potatoes were strongly associated with the Irish — who were seen as peasants — and (through the Irish) with Catholicism. Londoners and others spoke of the potato as 'Papist food' and came to belittle it for religious and loyalist reasons. Although it found a place as an accompaniment to meat and vegetables, it never challenged bread's superiority. Bread asserted itself unambiguously as the 'staff of life' and as the first and foremost staple food.

In England, bread's popularity was nationwide and was not confined to the wheat-growing regions alone. Even in those rural areas where farming was concentrated on the production of potatoes and other root crops, on dairy products or on mixed farming, demand for bread was paramount and English politicians in the nineteenth century were acutely aware of the economic and social importance of adequate bread supplies. The production, importation and distribution of wheat was central to political stability and occupied much of the time of Parliament.

In 1868 Caird estimated that the English and Scots had available to them 1¼ lb of bread and ½ lb of potatoes per head per day, whilst the Irish, in marked contrast, had 4½ lb of potatoes but only ¼ lb of bread per day. The same year, Lawes and Gilbert calculated that over the years 1852–3 to 1867–8, inclusive, average annual consumption of wheat per head in England and Wales was 6.1 bushels, whilst in Scotland it was

4.2 bushels and in Ireland 3 bushels. The average for the United Kingdom as a whole was calculated at 5.3 bushels. In 1880 they revised these figures to include a further 11-year period 1868–9 to 1879–80. The estimate for this last period was given as approximately 5.5 bushels per head per annum for the UK as a whole and, allowing for some probable downwards error in all periods, the overall UK consumption per head figure for the 28-year period was then estimated at 5⅔ bushels per annum.

The analyses of Caird and of Lawes and Gilbert are the best available for the period but both suffer from the fact that they estimate consumption on the basis of available supplies. They also fail to differentiate between regions within countries. However, across the kingdom as a whole, it is clear that demand for and consumption of bread was concentrated in the Celtic cities and throughout rural and urban England.

* * *

Given the importance of bread as a primary staple food, Robert Giffen could conceivably have come upon evidence of the paradox in either agricultural or industrial areas of Victorian Britain. For many reasons, however, the probability is that the phenomenon was observed in the city rather than in the countryside. Giffen had always been essentially concerned with urban affairs and in particular with the conditions of the industrial working class. He spent nearly all of his life working in two major cities — Glasgow and London — and throughout these years he wrote not about the life and conditions of the agricultural worker but about the plight of the urban poor and the fluctuations and improvements in their living standards. Although he served on several Royal Commissions and Committees with agricultural interests, he was never preoccupied with the problems of the rural labourer and his family.

Apart from Giffen's clear interest in the conditions of the urban worker, there are other reasons to suggest that his observation of paradox behaviour would have been made in the cities and larger towns of mid-Victorian Britain. First, the paradox statement referred to by Marshall implies a money economy in which bread, meat and other foods are purchased from professional food suppliers. Many agricultural workers, however, worked well away from towns and lived a very different life. They were either victims of the notorious truck system or were offered derisory wages together with an allocation of wheat, oats, potatoes and other vegetables by their landlord. The more fortunate would also be given a plot of land to cultivate for themselves. Under such conditions, the extent and sophistication of the 'money economy' implied by the paradox was absent. It is true that exceptionally in the south of England some four-fifths of the agricultural labourer's wages were paid in money (Hasbach 1966); however, the real wages of the southern agricultural worker were, on average, far lower than those of his more northerly counterparts, and he was often doing little more than subsisting on scraps.

A further reason for looking towards the cities rather than to rural areas for Giffen's paradox evidence relates to the 'purchase' of meat. In both northern and southern agricultural areas meat was seldom obtained from the butcher's shop. Agricultural workers made strenuous efforts to live off the land and to avoid the expensive services of butchers. In fact, most farm labourers kept an animal, usually a cow or pig, and did not buy meat in the sense implied by the paradox. Legitimate snaring of animals was sometimes allowed and poaching was widespread on large country estates, notwithstanding the frightening punishments which could be handed out to those caught in the act. In short, meat was bought by the farm worker only as a last resort.

Overall, perhaps the most significant reason why the paradox cannot be considered a phenomenon to be found among the agricultural labouring class is that the statement speaks of the poor curtailing their consumption, not only of meat but of the more expensive farinaceous foods. These relatively expensive luxuries were made available only to money earners in the towns and cities who were able to obtain and afford them. They formed no part of the diets of agricultural workers who were often paid in kind and whose money wages (if not their real wages) were significantly lower than those of the workers in the industrial towns and cities of the country.

The 1867 Royal Commission, which was appointed to examine the employment of children, young persons and women in agriculture, identified five geographical divisions of England, distinguished from each other by contrasting economic and social conditions which affected the way of life of the rural labourer:

> Roughly speaking, the south-eastern were the corn-producing coun-
> ties; the south-western were devoted to convertible husbandry,
> and thus formed the connecting link between the former and the
> purely pasture-counties of the west; the most prominent feature in
> the midlands was market gardening; while the north had no one
> common and distinctive agricultural characteristic. (Hasbach 1966,
> pp. 261–2)

In none of these five regions identified within the Report was the condition of the agricultural worker such that he was receiving all payment for his labour in money or receiving a wage substantial enough to allow him to vary shop purchases of 'bread, meat and the more expensive farinaceous foods' in response to changes in the price of bread. This again suggests that Giffen was not looking to rural England when he identified the paradox and that it was in the cities that such behaviour was to be observed at first hand. It is therefore to the industrial workers of mid-Victorian Britain that we must look for evidence of such 'perverse' demand.

*   *   *

The Industrial Revolution in Britain brought immense wealth to the major cities of the country and to the new capitalists, whose money and initiative had underpinned the new ventures. At the same time, the great influx of people into centres of commerce and manufacture brought overcrowding and poverty on a scale which had not hitherto been imagined.

By 1831, the population of Manchester — the first industrial city, though not officially a city until 1853 — had increased some six times in sixty years and by nearly 45 per cent over the previous decade. This massive expansion brought great wealth to the town but also depths of squalor which, at the time, were thought by some to be a necessary and unavoidable product of the cotton boom. However, the conditions of these new urban poor began to attract the attention of novelists and would-be social reformers in the 1840s, and led Engels to write his tract on *The Condition of the Working Class in England*.

Manchester was the focal point of Engels' research into the plight of the new working classes and was able to provide him with evidence of the atrocious conditions under which the vast majority of the town's population laboured in the middle years of the nineteenth century:

> The working-class quarters of the town are always badly laid out. Their houses are jerry-built and are kept in a bad state of repair. They are badly ventilated, damp and unhealthy. The workers are herded into the smallest possible space and in most cases all the members of (at the least) one family sleep together in a single room. The furnishings and household equipment are poor, and there are some workers' families where even the barest essentials are lacking. The clothing of the workers is also normally inadequate and many workers go about clad in rags. The workers' diet is generally poor and often almost inedible. From time to time many workers' families actually go short of food and in exceptional cases they actually die of hunger. (p. 87)

Looking in more detail at the diets of individual workers, Engels had concluded that they varied widely according to wages, with the very poor close to starvation:

> The better-paid workers — particularly when the whole family works in the factories — enjoy good food as long as they are in employment. They have meat every day and bacon and cheese for the evening meal. The lower-paid workers have meat only two or three times a week, and sometimes only on Sundays. The less meat they can afford, the more potatoes and bread they eat. Sometimes the meat consumed is cut down to a little chopped bacon mixed with the potatoes. The poorer workers can afford no meat at all and they eat cheese, bread, porridge and potatoes. The poorest of all are the Irish, for whom potatoes are the staple diet. (p. 85)

While Engels' subjective and sometimes inaccurate views of working-class life in Manchester in the 1840s have come under criticism in more recent years, there can be no doubt that the conditions under which the majority of the population were living at that time were hard and primitive by any standard. A survey by William Neild of the earnings and expenditure of 19 working-class families in Manchester and Dukinfield was published in 1841 by the Statistical Society of London. All families worked in the cotton industry and were, for the most part, skilled or semi-skilled, yet even here, among the employed, conditions were far from good. Expenditure on bread, flour and yeast typically represented some 35–40 per cent of total food expenditure for the poorer families, and purchases of so-called luxuries were at an absolute minimum. So far as the poorer, unskilled and partly employed or unemployed workers in other parts of Lancashire were concerned, life was no better. An inquiry into living conditions among the poor of Accrington (Somerville 1843) found that a family with a total income of 5s. 6d. a week was again spending 37 per cent of its total food budget on bread and flour, whilst a more 'prosperous' family, on 10s. a week, was spending 33 per cent. Neither family was eating any meat, although a few pennies were spent on bacon each week.

Throughout the decade, the need for change and reform was debated both inside and outside Parliament, but conditions improved only very slowly. In reality, the great wealth of Manchester continued to mask a large part of the appalling squalor faced by many of its citizens and it was this surface prosperity which attracted the attention of others. Nothing was allowed to stop the creation of 'a new order of businessmen, energetic, tough, proud, contemptuous of the old aristocracy and yet in some sense constituting an aristocracy themselves — an urban aristocracy — men who were beginning to seek political as well as economic power, power not only in Manchester but in the country as a whole' (Briggs 1963). As a consequence, there was little urgency in the limited programme of economic and social reform which was undertaken in the thirty years after 1850.

While conditions in Manchester were clearly reaching crisis point by the late 1840s, those in the less affluent parts of the capital were no better. In 1849 and 1850 Henry Mayhew carried out his now famous series of studies on the London poor, presenting them as letters to the *Morning Chronicle* — letters in which he highlighted the appalling lives and living conditions of the poorer sections of London society. He vividly illustrated the hardships faced by those who worked to advance the wealth of the capital. The plight of the workers in the East End of London

was particularly severe: the vast majority living with their
families in cramped conditions — often no more than a top back-
room in a dilapidated house — and crowded together in the
dismal courts which could be found throughout the area.
Mayhew found families of eight living in rooms of a few feet
square, with a small piece of matting on the floor, a bed, chair,
washing tub and a few pots and pans. The courts in which the
houses stood were themselves indescribably filthy and it was
not uncommon to find cesspools there which, in turn, infected
the water supplies and brought frequent outbreaks of cholera to
the town. Crime was also rife, and the police and medical
authorities were hard pressed to stop the atrocious conditions
from deteriorating further.

These terrible living conditions extended to diet. Mayhew
(1861) looked at the household expenditure on food of many
dock labourers' families and found desperately low levels of
nutrition:

> 'We buy most bread' said the wife 'and a bit of firing and I do manage
> on a Saturday night to get them a bit of meat for Sunday if I possibly
> can; but what with the soap, and one thing and another, that's the
> only day they do get a bit of meat, unless I've a bit given me. As for
> clothing, I'm sure I can't get them any unless I have that given me,
> poor little things. . . .'
> 'Yes, but we have managed to get a little bread lately' said the
> man. . . . 'We've known what it was sometimes to go without bread
> and coals in the depth of winter. . . . My children is very contented;
> give 'em bread, and they're as happy as all the world. That's one
> comfort. For instance, today we've had half a quartern loaf, and we
> had a piece left of last night's after I had come home. I had been
> earning some money yesterday. We had 2 oz. of butter, and I had
> this afternoon a quarter of an ounce of tea and a pennyworth of
> sugar. . . .' (Vol. 3, pp. 306–7)

Mayhew's evidence is made all the more convincing in that he
let the poorer sections of the working class speak for themselves
and so provided primary evidence of their way of life (this in
marked contrast to the considerable quantity of 'research by
observation' which became popular in the last twenty years of
the century). The dock labourers and their families, moreover,
were no special case in the London of 1850, and Mayhew's
accounts of the living conditions of many other groups only

served to highlight the equally miserable circumstances in which the vast majority of people were living. A casual labourer, for instance, who considered himself typical of many thousands of others, spent some 48 per cent of his food budget in any one week on bread, with only 4 per cent going on potatoes.

The problems of poverty and of casual labour persisted throughout the 1850s, into the 1860s and beyond. When times were particularly severe, the poor became increasingly desperate. Combinations of cyclical trade depression, severe winters and bad harvests were beginning to produce a greater, more menacing militancy: in 1853, the harvest failed disastrously; and the winter of 1854–5 was also particularly bad with the Thames freezing over. As the docks were blocked up and casual labour suspended, distress reached such a pitch that bread riots broke out in Whitechapel. Again, in 1860–1, an even more severe winter occurred (the Christmas Day temperature being some 17 degrees below freezing point), the harvest had failed and the price of wheat rose by 10s. per quarter. Once more, law and order broke down:

> On Tuesday much alarm was produced by an attack made on a large number of bakers' shops in the vicinity of Whitechapel Road and Commercial Road East. They were surrounded by a mob of about 30 or 40 in number who cleared the shops of the bread they contained and then decamped. On Wednesday night, however, affairs assumed a more threatening character, and acts of violence were committed. By some means it became known in the course of the afternoon that the dock labourers intended to visit Whitechapel in a mass, as soon as dusk set in, and that an attack would be made on all the provision shops in that locality. This led to a general shutting up of the shops almost throughout the East End, a precaution highly necessary, for between 7 and 9 p.m. 1000s congregated in the principal streets, and proceeded in a body from street to street. An attack was made upon many of the baking shops and eating houses, and every morsel of food was carried away. The mounted police of the district were present but it was impossible for them to act against so large a number of people. (*Morning Star*, 18 January, 1861)

Similar social unrest occurred during the hard winter of 1866–7 and it was not until the 1870s, when rising wages, better harvests and growing imports of wheat combined to improve living standards generally, that the bread riots began to recede as a potent social and political force.

The harsh economic climate of the 1860s brought no improvement in the living conditions of the poor. London housing conditions were by now scandalous. For the majority of the poor, overcrowding had now taken the form of living in 'tenements', particularly in those neighbourhoods which had once seen better days but were now run-down and dilapidated. These tenements were nothing more than houses or mansions, out of which the more affluent Londoners had long since moved. The old garden would often have been sold off as land for a factory, and the house itself would be let out to as many as fifteen families who would occupy one room each. The tenements were often in an appalling condition: no repairs would be carried out on rooms and staircases, and the forecourts were normally full of rubbish of every kind. Anything of value — iron railings, for example — would long ago have been 'removed' and sold.

The poor were living in conditions such as these all over the capital but the situation was by now particularly severe to the east of the city, in areas such as St George's, Whitechapel, Bethnal Green and Shoreditch (Hollingshead 1861). When they were not in tenements, the poor crowded together in more recently built houses comprising two small rooms about twelve feet square and a cupboard about half the size. Occupants of these 'courts' invariably shared the same public toilets and there could be as many as ten adults and children in each dwelling. Taken together, the tenements and courts provided the poor with no opportunity of living in anything other than squalor and misery.

So far as the people themselves were concerned, even for those fortunate enough to be in work, life was harsh and unforgiving. In 1863 the Sixth Report of the Medical Officer of the Privy Council on the food of the poorer labouring classes in England drew attention to the desperate circumstances of many Londoners. Needlewomen were subsisting on an average 2s. 7d. weekly and on a diet dominated by bread and potatoes. Half the families in the sample never bought any butcher's meat and those who did made their Sunday dinner from 1d. of sheep's brains or 1d. of black pudding. The Medical Officer concluded that those in the worst paid, indoor occupations in London were considerably worse fed than agricultural workers in terms of the carbonaceous and nitrogenous content of food.

In general, wages throughout the decade were often derisory: a Whitechapel dock labourer would earn no more than 3s. a day on the 'permanent list', and only 2s. 6d. a day on the 'casual list'; his wife could seek employment as a needlewoman, or perhaps as a cleaner, in order to bolster the family budget; and the older children would be lucky to find work in a match- or brush-making factory for a few pence a day. There was little or no social life. The husband and father would need to spend every penny of his wage on the home and family, and the wife's earnings would also have to help meet the family's bills. After a day's work, a miserable home awaited them, and with the children in bed, many couples visited local taprooms for a drink which was used to deaden the nerves against everyday life.

By 1870 the London authorities were beginning to realise that urgent action was needed to alleviate the housing problem and the living conditions of the poor. The Metropolitan Board of Works took action over the next ten years to relieve chronic overcrowding only to see a housing crisis of even greater proportions develop in the 1880s (Jones 1971). At the same time, the supply of casual labour continued to increase as periodic trade depressions reduced the amount of work available — a combination which ensured that improvements in wage rates were held back throughout the 1870s. However, after 1880 the situation was to improve as working-class diets benefited from the sustained fall in the prices of basic foodstuffs such as wheat and meat. The 1880s were, in fact, a crucial decade in the improvement of the English diet as the largest falls in food prices occurred then: the retail price of food in a typical workman's budget falling by 30 per cent in the ten years from 1877 to 1887 — the most significant price change of the century (Burnett 1966). Life was slowly beginning to improve but the very poor continued to struggle to achieve anything approaching a civilised standard of living.

The condition of the poorest labouring classes in all Victorian cities was a cause for concern through to the end of the nineteenth century. Studies as far apart as those of Mayhew and Charles Booth (1889) serve to illustrate how little was achieved in improving the lot of the residuum over forty years. The plight of the Victorian poor has been well documented and it serves no purpose to further restate what has been described in great detail by many social and economic historians. However, certain features of the life-style and conditions of these city dwellers are of particular importance.

First, there can be no doubt that, for those living in poverty in the major towns and cities of Britain, bread was the essential food. In his study of London's poor, Mayhew noted: 'Among *all*, however, I have heard statements of the blessing of cheap bread; always cheap *bread*. "There's nothing like bread", say the men, "it's not all poor people can get meat; but they *must* get bread"' (p. 228), and these same sentiments were to be reported by Booth and others many years later. The importance of bread in the diet is perhaps best illustrated by the fact that when it was in short supply or too expensive then bread riots occurred throughout the country. Bread was, quite simply, the one food that the poorer labouring classes in the inner cities refused to go without.

Second, the belief that potatoes were always an acceptable substitute for bread is not borne out by the facts. Bread was a ready-to-eat food which did not require cooking. Potatoes, in contrast, needed costly fuel to prepare, and the tenements and courts of the inner city often lacked cooking facilities entirely or at the very least made it difficult to prepare hot food. It was possible to have food cooked at the local baker's shop but this was expensive. There was also a lack of water (taps usually being located at the end of streets), which again made the preparation of potatoes difficult.

Pound for pound, bread offered a great deal more nutrition than potatoes and a quartern loaf provided a family with far more than its equivalent weight of potatoes. Again, the pound for pound comparative cost of bread and potatoes worked strongly against substitution. And overlaying all these problems of preparation, nutritional value and cost-effectiveness was the cultural dimension — an almost mystical regard for bread as being the most important food and a contempt for the potato, particularly in London, as being 'Irish' and 'Papist'. Potatoes, in short, were acceptable to the bread-eaters mainly as an accompaniment to meat but did not seriously challenge bread as the staple food and were never a wholly acceptable substitute to the urban worker when bread was scarce.

The prejudice against the potato is illustrated by Mayhew's research into the diets of London scavengers. Whilst all those interviewed (62 interviewees) spent heavily on bread, when asked about their potato purchases, 28 respondents spent nothing at all each week on potatoes and only 1 spent as much as a shilling. Clearly, when meat was not available (and many scavengers could not afford meat) then very few potatoes were purchased. Bread, in contrast, was purchased in all circumstances as the essential staple food.

The preference for bread in the cities of Victorian Britain is beyond question, and it is surely to these cities that we must look for evidence of the paradox. Giffen himself lived in only two cities during his lifetime. As a young man, he worked for several years in Glasgow before entering journalism but by far the greater part of his life was spent in London, firstly as a journalist then as a civil servant. Whilst Glasgow workers showed a preference for bread, London's belief in bread as the only 'civilised' staple food was much stronger. Set in the heart of wheat-growing southern England, London's prejudice against 'Irish' potatoes was far more intense than that of the cities to the north where the bread culture, though strong, had been tempered by greater exposure to Celtic immigration and values.

If Giffen observed the paradox at first hand, therefore, it is most likely that he would have witnessed such behaviour in London itself. Certainly, London had an abundance of the 'poorer labouring classes' referred to in the paradox statement, and poverty was to be found in all parts of the city. As a journalist, a writer on social and economic matters and a professional statistician concerned with trade data, Giffen would have been well informed about the conditions of the London working class and about the hardships suffered by the residuum in the second half of the nineteenth century.

It has already been shown that conditions most likely to produce evidence of the paradox were those to be found in the towns and cities of Britain between 1850 and 1880. Robert Giffen, however, arrived in London only in 1862, at the age of 25, to take up a position as sub-editor of the *Globe* newspaper. If he himself was witness to paradox behaviour then it is to the period 1862–80 that we should look for evidence of such 'perverse' patterns of consumption on the part of the poor.

Paradox behaviour could clearly have been produced by any upwards movement in bread prices over these years, and records show that such increases did, in fact, occur. However, the pattern is very uneven over the period. Bread prices were static or falling throughout 1862 and 1863, and it was not until 1864 that a price rise was recorded (for only one quarter of the year). However, from January 1865, prices began to climb and continued to rise for the next three years. The price of a quartern loaf went from 5½d. in 1864 to 9d. in March 1868, and this steep increase in the price of the most essential staple food was one of the worst recorded in the second half of the nineteenth century, only the three-year price rise from 1851–4 being steeper. After March 1868 prices fell away significantly but rose again in 1871 when the average price of wheat per Imperial Quarter increased by over 17 per cent. Prices climbed slightly through 1872 and 1873, but 1874 saw the beginning of a sustained fall in prices.

Over the period 1862–80, therefore, the years 1865–8 produced a most dramatic and sustained increase in bread prices — an increase which put the food budgets of the poor under severe pressure. By 1867, after two years of real hardship, the mood of the working classes was turning ugly. The 1866–7 winter had been particularly bad, and by January 1867 the food situation was no longer tolerated. There were bread riots in Deptford and Greenwich, and bakers' shops were attacked by mobs demanding an end to dear bread. Prices did not come down, however. Agricultural workers went on strike (complaining about the high price of bread) and this put further upward pressure on town prices. At the same time, there was an unstable political situation. The second Reform Act was moving through Parliament and there was considerable trouble with the Irish. In June, anti-popery riots broke out in Birmingham, followed by 'Fenian outrages' in Manchester and Holborn in September. The potato, a theoretical substitute, had few friends in London and was in any event still much dearer than bread, pound for pound.

By December 1867, the poor had had to face nearly three years of bread price rises. To add to their problems, the 1867 harvest failed badly with the result that the three months from December 1867 to March 1868 saw the steepest increase in the price of a quartern loaf since 1854. By the end of the first quarter of 1868, the price had reached 9*d*. and the poor were in dire straits.

With bread prices so high, it was reasonable to expect that the poorer sections of society would be forced to cut back on their consumption of bread. This expectation was made all the greater in view of the fact that, in general terms, 1868 wages could be anywhere from 15 per cent to 25 per cent lower than those of 1865, and for actual productive purposes, perhaps 25 per cent to 30 per cent lower (*The Statist*, March 1868). However, there is evidence that cutbacks in bread consumption did not occur.

In March 1868 James Caird read a paper to the Statistical Society 'On the agricultural statistics of the United Kingdom'. The paper marked the publication of a *Blue Book* which contained the agricultural returns for 1867, obtained from nearly half a million people on every farm, large and small, in Great Britain. The report was to be the precursor of many future statistical analyses, published at public expense, and it paved the way for a far more sophisticated understanding of agricultural progress and activity.

In looking at the average yearly consumption of wheat and flour during the previous five years (some 20,800,000 quarterns), Caird was interested to know to what extent demand had been influenced by changes in price:

> . . . On this point, I had the advantage of hearing the opinion of Mr Newmarch, lately expressed in this room, in which I generally concur. It was to the effect that the consumption of bread is very constant, that everything is given up before bread, and that bread being the staff of life it must be had by the people whatever the price may be. This view is confirmed by inquiries which I have since made among some of the leading bakers in the most densely peopled quarters of Whitechapel in the east, and the Harrow Road in the north-west, one of whom has been thirty years in business and has now three shops in a district entirely inhabited by the working classes. Their testimony is that the consumption of bread at present is very large, for, although dear, it is still the cheapest article of food within reach of the poor, the next substitute, potatoes, being scarce and very dear. (p. 134)

At a time of lower wages, of bread riots and attacks on bakers' shops, therefore, Caird's inquiries among bakers whose customers were exclusively poor and working class showed that purchases of bread were 'at present very large', suggesting not only that bread sales had remained high but that they had, if anything, increased — and this at a time when the quartern loaf was costing between 8*d*. and 9*d*. Caird had, in fact, come across a paradox.

Despite this primary evidence, Caird remained sceptical: 'Still, I feel persuaded that price has some influence, and that the rise of the quartern loaf of household bread from 5½*d*. in 1864 to 9*d*., the present price, must produce some effect on the total consumption. With that belief, I will assume that every 10 % of additional price on the loaf, diminishes the consumption by at least 1 %' (p. 134). Caird, in short, could not bring himself to believe that the paradox was real — a paradox which went against the conventional view of demand which argued that as the price of a commodity rises (substantially in this case) then demand must to some degree be adversely affected.

One year later, in March 1869, Caird published a second paper 'On the agricultural statistics of the United Kingdom' and returned to the question of the price elasticity of demand for bread: 'It will, perhaps, be remembered that I assumed every 10 % of additional price on the crop would diminish the consumption by 1 %; and as bread had risen over 50 %, I reckoned the saving at 5 %'. In fact, on the basis of 1868 statistics, Caird found that 'the very severe pinch of an increase of price of fully one-half diminished the use of it by only one-twentieth' (p. 62). At first sight, Caird's results suggest that he was right to be suspicious of the Whitechapel bakers' sales estimates and that demand for bread had, indeed, been affected by the price rises, even if only marginally. However, this was not the case, for while Caird's original paradox behaviour had been observed only among the very poor living in the East End of London, his 1869 paper was based on statistics showing the *national* consumption of bread. Nationally, consumption may well have fallen by 5 per cent in response to a 50 per cent increase but this was an aggregate statistic and would have masked the fact that, when disaggregated, bread consumption among the urban poor could be shown to have *increased* as Caird's bakers had claimed. Caird's 1869 analysis therefore only served to hide the White-chapel paradox.

There is, in fact, good reason to believe that James Caird had come across the paradox. Indeed, it is difficult to deny its existence. Bread prices were at their highest for a generation, bread riots were commonplace and wage rates were falling, yet Whitechapel bakers were reporting an increase in the consumption of bread in an exclusively working-class area. The explanation for such behaviour is not hard to find. Having been faced with rising bread prices for some three years, and with all opportunities to postpone purchases of other essentials gone, families would at first have cut back on the quantities of 'meat and other farinaceous foods' which they normally purchased. Eventually, however, as bread prices continued to rise, the quantities of these other items which it was possible to buy after meeting the cost of bread would have become so small that it would have paid (in nutritional terms) to purchase an additional loaf, whatever its price, rather than negligible amounts of meat, potatoes and other luxuries. In short, the classic exception to the law of demand was, in 1868, a rational purchase decision taken by many thousands of people living in acute poverty in the East End of London.

*   *   *

In the late 1860s, at this time of suffering and deprivation for many thousands of people, Robert Giffen was establishing his career in London. In 1867 he had joined the Statistical Society and was working as Assistant Editor of both the *Daily News* and the *Fortnightly Review*. It was in this year also that his first major article 'The reduction of the National Debt' was written. The paper, far from being pessimistic as to the condition of the country, was complacent about existing wealth and future prospects. Giffen made great play on the fact that the national wealth had trebled since 1845 — a testament to the effectiveness of free trade, his great passion. It would, of course, have served none of Giffen's political interests to focus on the appalling misery of the residuum who, after two years of rising prices and increasing unemployment, were now becoming a major political, social and economic problem.

If he had been unaware of the conditions facing the mass of

the poor in 1867, he was rapidly disabused. Moreover, it was the East End of London which was beginning to attract most attention. On 2 January 1868 his newspaper, the *Daily News*, ran an editorial on 'East London distress' in which the desperation of the people living along the Thames 'where poverty and want have formed their miserable and cheerless home' was graphically described. On 11 January a second editorial demanded that action be taken to relieve the acute distress of the people of the East End. As Assistant Editor on the paper, Giffen could not have remained unaware of the poverty which existed only a few miles from the offices in which he worked.

The impact on Giffen was clear. Towards the end of 1867 he published a further article 'Financial questions for the reformed Parliament' and the tone was entirely different to that of his earlier paper. He now launched an attack on the complacency and prejudice of the rich in Parliament, in particular on their determination to ensure that the greater part of the tax burden fell on 'necessaries' which were essential to the very survival of the poor. Giffen was clearly pressing for a more egalitarian system of taxation and in particular attacking the view, then in fashion, that the aggregate taxation of the working classes should be equal in amount to the aggregate taxation of the rest of the community.

> That it is monstrous appears most clearly to arise from the fact that the taxation of small incomes comes into collision with the primary duty of their possessors — the maintenance of themselves and their families in life and health. It is only the sum beyond this minimum, whatever it is, which individuals in any class have really got to dispose of at their pleasure, and only upon the surplus should the taxes be laid. (p. 715)

Some months earlier, Giffen had been writing: 'A little turn of the financial screw would diminish in no degree the annual savings of capital, though it might to an imperceptible extent diminish the consumption and perhaps the enjoyments of the people' (1867a, p. 274).

The East London crisis had influenced Giffen and focused his attention far more on the poor than on the 'affluent working class' to which he referred in the National Debt paper. The following year, Giffen began work for Goschen, then President of the Poor Law Board, on the Local Taxation Report to the Treasury — a report which again brought Giffen close to the poverty in which a sizeable part of the population was living. Any residual complacency which he had felt about the (relative) success of free trade in the years since 1846 must have been quickly tempered by a greater realisation that, in absolute terms, the poor were often still living in extreme distress on a day-to-day basis.

The *Daily News* continued to report on the deteriorating situation in the East End of London throughout 1868. On 10 August an editorial examined the 'high prices of the necessaries of life' in the capital and the exploitation which was occurring. However, the paper refused to condemn the tradesmen alone, arguing that they 'have been much blamed for making the best of their advantages, though in doing so they have only acted as tradesmen should'. Three days later, on 13 August, a further editorial noted that the situation was by then becoming so bad in the East End that unemployed Millwall labourers were emigrating to avoid starvation. On 4 September the paper again returned to the subject, highlighting the appalling conditions of the common lodging houses in the area. Throughout this time, Giffen was working in the editorial offices of the newspaper, and was seeing confirmation of his earlier description of the living conditions of the very poor as 'little better than a sort of death in life' (1867b).

The three years after 1865 had seen the situation of the casual labourer (of which there were many in the docklands of East London) continue to worsen, reaching a peak of misery and deprivation in March 1868, when the price of a quartern loaf had risen to 9*d*. In the summer of the same year, however, prospects began to improve. On 29 July the *Daily News* forecast cheaper bread in the light of predictions that the harvest would be far better than in recent years, and by February 1869 the same newspaper was announcing that, while conditions remained bad, the worst was by that time certainly over.

In spite of the marginally better living conditions, the suffering of 1865–8 had left its mark on Giffen. In 1869 he published 'Mr Gladstone's work in finance' in which he drew together the two themes of his 1867 papers, arguing that whilst the country had never been more prosperous, the unequal distribution of wealth was forcing many millions to live in abject misery:

> The conception of a vast manufacturing community, well fed, and housed, and clothed, living in comfort — what would even have been thought affluence only a century ago — was hardly thought possible till people witnessed the growth of such a community almost before their eyes. But . . . to distribute the accumulated wealth of the country more evenly, to cause it to be shared more and more largely by the mass — especially those who are just struggling out of the borders of pauperism — are objects of paramount importance, which might be worth, if need were, the weighting of the balance of taxation in favour of the poor. (p. 104)

Giffen, in essence, was now arguing that whilst the gains from free trade were indisputable, the distribution of the wealth it had created was unacceptable in humanitarian terms, and the system of taxation should be modified and used to ensure a more equitable spread of benefits across the community as a whole. Giffen's involvement with Goschen in research into Poor Law administration, his work as Assistant Editor on the *Daily News* and his attendance at meetings of the Statistical Society where men such as James Caird were often highlighting the poverty and misery of the times — all had a major influence in convincing him that, in 1867–8, the poorer labouring classes in the large cities were close to starvation and that the Government had to find a remedy through taxation and the redistribution of wealth.

For Giffen, the 1870s saw many of the injustices of the late 1860s put right. The economy grew stronger and imports of cheap American wheat guaranteed that, even when the UK harvest failed, bread prices would not rise. The middle years of the 1870s indeed saw a substantial fall in commodity prices, a theme taken up by Giffen in an 1879 paper to the Statistical Society. In this paper, however, he made passing reference to the 1865–8 experience:

> One bad harvest among several good ones may not have much visible influence, but a succession of them is recognised as a potent cause of mischief. The usual explanation has been that the bad harvest, leading to a high price of bread, causes direct distress among the masses of consumers, that their purchases of staple

manufactures fall off, that the people in the trades so affected also become poor and so by a quick round all trades become impoverished. If a second bad harvest follows the first, and a third the second, these evil effects are aggravated, and affairs at last come to be very bad. (p. 46)

This, argued Giffen, had historically been the case but the three bad harvests of 1875, 1876 and 1877 had caused no increase in bread prices owing to the fact that the UK harvest had by then become so unimportant compared to aggregate foreign importations that a 25 per cent deficiency in the crop over three consecutive years was of little or no consequence. The 9*d*. quartern loaf of 1868 had, in real terms, gone for ever.

In 1883, Giffen gave his inaugural address as President of the Statistical Society on 'The progress of the working classes in the last half century' and made it clear that, in his opinion, the improvements in living standards, which had by then been achieved, had been so great that even the poor were immeasurably richer than those of earlier generations. The concern he had shown in 1867–8 about the living conditions of the poor — 'a sort of death in life' — had largely gone, and although his paper, when published in the Society's journal, caused protests from many quarters, Giffen never again really believed that the scale of distress witnessed in the 1860s was in evidence to any significant extent after 1880.

The exceptional poverty of the 1860s was referred to again by Giffen on a later occasion. The British Library of Political and Economic Science holds the manuscript of an undated letter written but never submitted by Giffen to the Editor of *The Times* on the subject of 'The unemployed' (Giffen Collection , Vol. 3, Item 24). Referring to a debate, led by Lord Salisbury, on the need for an enquiry into London unemployment, Giffen wrote:

Pauperism until the last year or two has not been increasing but diminishing, not only in the metropolis but all over the country. We are told that the pauperism figures are misleading: that in consequence of the more stringent application of the workhouse test there is less legal pauperism but the poverty itself has increased; and so on. But this contention is manifestly unsound. Real poverty, if at all increasing seriously, would overbear any workhouse test, as it has done in past times — as it did so lately in 1867 and 1868 in the metropolis itself when the ship-building strike in the East End

swelled the ranks of pauperism at that time; as it did in Lancashire
during the cotton famine. (pp. 3–4)

Giffen clearly believed that the poverty of the 1860s had been far
worse than that of any other recent period. Given that the
paradox appears among those who are little more than one step
removed from the workhouse and close to being officially
classified as paupers, then the 1860s, more than any other
Victorian decade, provided the conditions under which it was
most likely to occur.

What evidence we have points to the fact that the 'Giffen
paradox' could be seen in the East End of London in 1867–8 and
that James Caird had come across such behaviour in Whitechapel at the time when he carried out his informal interviews
with the bakers of the area. Moreover, it was at this time, more
than at any other, that Robert Giffen would have become aware
of the paradox and would then have been able to challenge
Marshall some years later, when the controversies surrounding
the 'universal' law of demand were being discussed by Nicholson
and others. At the very least, the events of 1867–8 show that the
paradox is something more than a purely theoretical possibility
and that the conditions can exist under which such behaviour is
imposed on many thousands of people whose need to survive
drives them to live exclusively on the cheapest staple food
available to them.

The events in Whitechapel would have been seen quite
differently by Caird and Giffen. Caird was conventional and, as
already shown, sceptical of behaviour which appeared not to
conform to the received wisdom of the day. Higher prices, to
Caird, necessarily led to falls in demand, and his later aggregate
statistical data suggested he was right to believe that this was so.
Giffen, on the other hand, was a lover of paradox and quite
prepared to accept evidence of behaviour which ran counter to
the dogma of so-called 'experts'. He was, moreover, always
suspicious of conclusions drawn from aggregate statistical
analysis, arguing that 'no statistical table almost can be used
without qualification'. For this reason, he would not have been
prepared to accept anything other than disaggregated statistical
data before agreeing to any universal law of demand. For Robert
Giffen, the Whitechapel phenomenon — to be found, no doubt,

in the deprived areas of other inner cities — would have been
seen as a paradox created by the special circumstances of 1885–8.

References

Booth, C. (1889) *Life and Labour of the People of London*, Williams and
   Norgate.
Briggs, A. (1963) *Victorian Cities*, Odhams Press.
Burnett, J. (1966) *Plenty and Want*, Nelson.
Caird, J. (1868) 'On the agricultural statistics of the United Kingdom',
   Journal of the Statistical Society, Vol. 31 (June), pp. 127–45.
Caird, J. (1869) 'On the agricultural statistics of the United Kingdom',
   Journal of the Statistical Society, Vol. 32 (March), pp. 61–77.
Dwyer, G.P. and Lindsay, C.M. (1984) 'Robert Giffen and the Irish
   potato', *American Economic Review*, Vol. 74 (March), pp. 188–92.
Engels, F. (1845) *Die Lage Der Arbeitenden Klasse in England*, translated
   and edited by W.O. Henderson and W.H. Chaloner, Blackwell (2nd
   edn, 1971).
Giffen, R. (1867a) 'The reduction of the National Debt' reprinted in
   Essays in Finance, 1st Series (1880), George Bell and Sons, pp. 259–79.
Giffen, R. (1867b) 'Financial questions for the reformed Parliament',
   Fortnightly Review, Vol. 8 (Old Series) (July-December), pp. 711–25.
Giffen, R. (1869) 'Mr Gladstone's work in finance', *Fortnightly Review*,
   Vol. 11, pp. 101–16.
Giffen, R. (1879) 'On the fall of prices of commodities in recent years',
   Journal of the Statistical Society, Vol. 42 (March), pp. 36–68.
Giffen, R. (1883) 'The progress of the working classes in the last half
   century', *Journal of the Statistical Society*, Vol. 46, pp. 593–622.
Hasbach, W. (1966) *A History of the English Agricultural Labourer*, Nelson.
Hollingshead, J. (1861) *Ragged London in 1861*, Smith Elder & Co.
Jones, G.S. (1971) *Outcast London*, Oxford University Press.
Lawes, J.B. and Gilbert, J.H. (1868) 'On the home produce, imports and
   consumption of wheat', *Journal of the Royal Agricultural Society*, 2nd
   Series, Vol. 4, pp. 359–96.
Lawes, J.B. and Gilbert, J.H. (1880) 'On the home produce, imports,
   consumption and price of wheat over twenty-eight (or twenty-seven)
   harvest years 1852–53 to 1879–80 inclusive', *Journal of the Statistical
   Society*, Vol. 43 (June), pp. 313–31.
Mayhew, H. (1861) *London Labour and the London Poor*, Vol. 3. (The
   London Street Folk), Griffen, Bohn & Co.; republished by Dover
   Publications, 1968.
Neild, W. (1842) 'Comparative statement of the income and expendi-
   ture of certain families of the working classes in Manchester and

Dukinfield in the years 1836 and 1841', *Journal of the Statistical Society of London*, Vol. 4 (January), pp. 320–34.

Salaman, R.N. (1949) *The History and Social Influence of the Potato*, Cambridge University Press.

Samuelson, P.A. (1964) *Economics* (5th edn), McGraw Hill.

Somerville, A. (1843) 'A letter to the farmers of England on the relationship of manufactures and agriculture by one who has whistled at the plough'.

CHAPTER 7

Before and After Giffen

Having looked in some detail at the circumstances surrounding 'Giffen's' paradox, the phenomenon can now be viewed in a much wider context. This chapter examines economic conditions and the literature relating to the paradox through the nineteenth century to the Second World War.

Giffen was not the first to notice the special behaviour of individuals and families with regard to food purchases. As early as 1699, Charles Davenant had argued that the demand for food was such that shortages were capable of producing significant changes in the demand for other commodities — changes which in turn had consequences for the rest of the economy. Later, Engel (1857), primarily on the basis of a budget study of 153 Belgian families carried out by Ducpetiaux (1855), proposed a law of consumption, namely that 'the poorer a family, the greater the proportion of its total expenditure that must be devoted to the provision of food'. Engel also argued that the proportion of income spent on food was without question the best indicator of the standard of living of any individual, group or country. By 1895 the proposition that food expenditure, as a proportion of total expenditure, increases as real income declines had been generally accepted and was not at all controversial. Giffen's paradox, therefore, makes no remarkable claim in suggesting that expenditure on food makes the first claim on the income of the poor or that, *in extremis*, it will take almost all income.

Marshall was also mistaken in believing Giffen to have been the first to remark on the paradox. Rashid (1979) has pointed out that as early as 1800 the Reverend Henry Beeke, the first Oxford professor to lecture on political economy, wrote to Lord Sidmouth in an attempt to persuade him that Britain had no reason to expect that corn would become scarce in the immediate future:

> It may at first appear a little paradoxical, and I once thought it so; but the Fact I believe is indisputable and the Reasons for it are easily explained; that in all times of Dearness, there is an Increase in the consumption of whatever forms the Basis of the Food of the People, so long as by retrenching all other expense in Provisions they can possibly find Money to purchase it. They do not understand the Arts of Economical Cookery, they have not Utensils for it, their Stomachs are not used to novelties. With us the Consumption of Bread always increases when their Money, if divided, will not purchase an addition of Meat to the Diet which they cannot abandon. And this is true even when Bread is become in comparison far more costly. The Bakers constantly assert that they sell most Bread when Provisions are very dear. The Butchers as generally assert that they sell most Meat when Bread is cheap.

Some few years later, in 1804, Simon Gray wrote (and in 1815 published) *The Happiness of States: Or an Inquiry Concerning Population, the Modes of Subsisting and Employing It, and the Effects of All on Human Happiness*. Chapter 5, Book 7 of this work — 'A rise in the price of bread corn, beyond a certain pitch, tends to increase the consumption of it' — argued that as prices increase beyond a certain point, the poorer working classes are obliged not to cut their purchases of bread but to increase them:

> It will be asked, why do they not buy something else than this very thing, which is grown so dear? The answer is obvious. They have it not in their power to buy anything else. The reason why this part of the population lives so much on Bread is, that their incomes are not sufficient for them to buy meat etc. even when bread is cheap. All the surplus after buying bread, and some necessary articles of clothing, is laid out, indeed, on these more desirable species of food. But in proportion as bread rises in price, this surplus decreases, till at length there is no surplus at all; and in many cases the whole of their earnings is not even sufficient to buy the quantity of bread and potatoes necessary, without the assistance of the parish. . . . (pp. 505–6)
> . . . By raising the price of bread corn, thus, far from making the people live less on that necessary, as so many, who have not thoroughly considered the matter, imagine, we force them to live more on it; and beyond a certain price, almost entirely. (pp. 509–10)

Both Beeke and Gray were convinced of the existence of

behaviour relating to bread consumption which ran counter to the general law of demand, but neither claim was supported by empirical evidence. This is not surprising as quantitative analysis was then a rarity, although there was often considerable sympathy expressed over the plight of the poor. Coincidentally, however, the first two budget studies into the living conditions of the working class had been carried out in the 1780s and 1790s.

In 1795 David Davies, a Berkshire clergyman, edited 127 budgets of the labouring poor living in his own parish and elsewhere, which had been collected by himself and by correspondents in other parts of the country since 1787. Some two years after Davies' book appeared, Frederick Eden finished a three-volume study in which the budgets of some 60 agricultural workers were included as an appendix to the work. Eden had been encouraged in his research by the very high prices for corn and other provisions which had been in evidence in 1794–5 as a result of the failure of the wheat crop and the need to finance the war against France.

From the evidence gathered by both Davies and Eden there is little doubt that by 1795 white bread formed the cornerstone of the diet of the English rural labourer — indeed, many households in the samples consumed bread and no other starches, such as potatoes or oatmeal. The work of these two pioneers of empirical studies into working-class budgets is too casual, data collection too uncontrolled, and the samples taken too small to allow for further analysis but they do at least provide convincing evidence of the central importance of bread in the English working-class diet at the time when Beeke and Gray were laying claim to an early version of the Giffen paradox.

Koenker (1977) has questioned whether, notwithstanding this dependence on bread, there was any firm evidence to suggest that demand for bread was 'Giffen' in the late eighteenth century. His attempt to analyse the primitive Davies and Eden data, however, only served to confirm that the material was not capable of allowing anything other than broad generalisation. Against this, Beeke and Gray were clearly in no doubt and thought it not at all paradoxical, but a simple and easily observed fact of life, that the poor, at that time, were obliged to eat greater quantities of bread as the price of a loaf increased. Their view is given added weight when it is remembered that by

1801 wheat was 119s. 6d. per quarter, the price of a 4 lb loaf was
1s. 2d. and wages averaged 1s. to 2s. per day. All the earnings of
a poor family simply had to go on food in order to survive.

Given Beeke's eminence as an Oxford professor, it is likely
that his views on the demand for bread would have been widely
known in the early 1800s. Certainly, Lord Sidmouth knew of
them and could well have taken such views into the House of
Lords. This in itself raises an interesting possibility with regard
to the debate leading up to the introduction of the Corn Laws in
1815, for the implications of paradox behaviour were highly
significant in so far as Government policy was concerned. In
essence, Beeke was claiming that the demand for wheat on the
part of the poor would not in fact decrease as the price of bread
rose but would rather increase up to the point at which famine
conditions prevailed. This eminent opinion would have been of
the greatest value to the agricultural interests, who were
determined to maintain the high prices for wheat which they
had enjoyed during the Napoleonic Wars and who were
seeking, through legislation, to secure the highest possible
prices consistent with substantial consumer demand.

The Government was committed to maintaining agricultural
prices at a level high enough to make farming profitable (Ashton
1948). The squirearchy, however, was concerned with something more — the maximisation of profitability. In fact, the 1815
Act prohibited the release of foreign wheat to millers so long as
the price at home was below 80s. a quarter, effectively
prohibiting relief from abroad until conditions approached those
of famine. In pressing for so high a price, the farming lobby
would have been encouraged in the belief that they could expect
buoyant consumer demand for wheat up to the 'famine price' of
80s. a quarter.

The introduction of the Corn Laws brought some insurance to
the farmer and landowners, with regard to the return on wheat
crops, but little comfort to the newly-emerging town workers. In
the years up to 1840, the diet of the new industrial working class
showed little improvement over the years of the Napoleonic
Wars. Even for the new industrial elite — the skilled Mancunians
working in the cotton industry — life was difficult. In 1833, the
Factory Commissioners described the diet of a Manchester
spinner's family from whom they had taken evidence:

Breakfast consisted of porridge or bread and milk, lined with flour or oatmeal on weekdays and tea and bread and butter on Sundays. Potatoes, bacon and bread (usually white) were provided for dinner on weekdays and a little fresh meat but no butter eggs or pudding on Sundays. Supper on weekdays consisted of oatmeal porridge and milk, sometimes potatoes and milk. On Sundays (but never on weekdays) a little bread and cheese was sometimes provided. When eggs fell to ½d. each the spinner's wife occasionally fried some with bacon.

Despite the relatively privileged situation of this family, 37 per cent of the weekly expenditure on food for the husband, wife and five children went on bread, and it is not difficult to imagine the straits in which the less fortunate unskilled or unemployed found themselves at this time. In his report to the Poor Law Commissioners in July 1835, Dr Kay, who had made a close study of Manchester factory operatives, attributed their poor health and physique to a diet which consisted of tea, bread, boiled potatoes with fried bacon and, occasionally, meat and spirits. Overall, the 1830s was a decade of deprivation and misery for the new industrial worker.

There can be little doubt that the dietary conditions to be found in the towns of England over the first half of the nineteenth century provided every opportunity for what we now know as Giffen's paradox to have occurred among those whose food budgets pushed them close to starvation. The difference between such paradox behaviour and that which Giffen observed in the later part of the century is only relative, for while Giffen saw the poor giving up purchases of meat and other farinaceous luxuries in order to increase their purchases of dearer bread, the poor of the 1830s, having no meat or biscuits to give up, would have been sacrificing purchases of what, to them, were the equivalent luxuries of cheese, sugar, milk and tea. As Beeke and Gray knew, when wheat was dear and men were cheap paradox behaviour — seen by Gray as 'plain substantial fact' — was easily found among the poor.

The harsh living standards faced by the majority of workers in the first half of the century improved only slowly until the 1870s. Conditions tended to see-saw between prosperity and depression: years of improvement being offset quickly by sharp setbacks. From time to time, the prices of necessaries increased dramatically. The worst harvest between 1848 and 1868 was in 1853 – a harvest twice as bad as the 1867 failure — and the price of bread in 1853–4 increased significantly. However, the effects of the price increases were somewhat mitigated by the fact that the harvest failed at a time when trade was otherwise good and wages relatively high. After 1853, there were ten good harvest years, with only two below average, but the years 1865–8 were to prove disastrous. A more sustained improvement followed in the 1870s, and after 1880 the social and economic circumstances of the industrial working class began to improve significantly as cheaper food, higher wages and major advances in housing and sanitary conditions combined to raise the standard of living. Even after 1880, however, the residuum was still doing little more than surviving.

William Booth (1890) spoke of the 'submerged tenth' of the population — three million people — who were always pauperised and degraded. Giffen himself was more cautious, estimating that this 'destitute army' comprised one in five manual labourers, i.e. 1,800,000 people representing 6 in 100 of the total population. Chamberlain thought the figure was much higher, around four million, but had included more people seen to be at the border line of destitution. No matter how the calculations were made, however, it was beyond dispute that a significant part of the population was seeing little improvement in living conditions, whilst standards elsewhere were beginning to rise through the 1880s.

Equally, there can be little doubt that, for those who could be described as poor but not destitute, conditions had changed for the better. In 1889 Charles Booth had begun his series of studies on London life with an examination of poverty in East London. Looking at the diets of the 'very poor' casual labourers (Class B in his study) and at those of the 'poor' (Classes C and D), he was able to illustrate how difficult day-to-day living remained for the underprivileged. Nevertheless, for groups B, C and D little more than 20 per cent of total food expenditure now went on bread and flour — a significant fall from the percentages recorded before 1880 and an improvement which worked against wide observation of the Giffen paradox. Indeed, a few years later, Giffen was to agree with Bowley (1895) that 'actual want is now only the lot of a small proportion of the nation (though intrinsically a large number) and comfort is within the reach of increasing masses of workmen'. Giffen clearly believed that evidence of paradox behaviour was, by the 1890s, only to be found deep within the residuum among those at the very edges of survival. This was to have been expected as living conditions generally improved and as the importance of bread within the overall diet began to recede. By the turn of the century, dietary patterns were beginning to show marked change.

In 1901 Rowntree carried out a study of living conditions in York. Although bread was baked in the home (very much a Yorkshire custom) rather than bought in the shop, it is still possible to use his findings to calculate the percentage of total food expenditures which went on baking bread. In the category of families whose total weekly earnings were under 26s. per week, a household consisting of father, mother and five children and with total earnings of 17s. 6d. per week was spending, on average, 28.8 per cent weekly on bread in 1899 and 1900. However, a married labourer with three children, earning 15s. per week, was spending only 20 per cent on bread in April 1900 at a time when the family was heavily in debt. Another family budget shows expenditure on bread at only 18.5 per cent of the total food budget. Overall, Rowntree's data suggest an average percentage expenditure on bread for the poorest workers in the 20–25 per cent range.

This falling expenditure on bread, when expressed as a percentage of all household food expenditure, is confirmed elsewhere. A 1903 Board of Trade report on urban workers' budgets showed that expenditure on meat was by then heavier than that on bread and that, in overall terms, expenditure on protein was growing at the expense of carbohydrate foods. In 1904 the Board of Trade again studied dietary patterns across the country and found that, in the poorest families living on less than 25s. per week, expenditure on bread as a percentage of all food expenditure was, on average, 21 per cent. However, Roberts (1971) has made the point that in Salford, for example, a good 20 per cent of the whole population lived on an income of 18s. or less each week, and there is no statistical evidence of the expenditure on bread as a percentage of total food expenditure for this most underprivileged group.

Whilst household diets were, statistically at least, showing a

marked improvement over those of some fifty years earlier, the
benefits of a more varied diet often came to the father but not to
other members of the family. Despite higher incomes and
improved conditions generally, the diet of married women was
more often than not based on bread and tea. Children also, as
Russell (1905) pointed out, often subsisted on little more than
bread, margarine and tea, supplemented perhaps by a few small
luxuries at the beginning of the week.

Yet it was still the case that families were forced to revert to
plainer, cheaper diets when the household income dropped
significantly. Roberts (1971), describing his Edwardian child-
hood as the son of a Salford shopkeeper, makes the point:

> When bad times came our tick customers at the shop were, of course,
> forced to adjust their diet: it began to fall off in quality, quantity and
> variety. Some made the change-down with great reluctance. Often
> a housewife would go on buying the cake or biscuits her family
> had grown used to in prosperity at the expense of plainer, more
> nourishing but less palatable fare. Then, forced by degrees to give
> them up, she went in for small quantities of jam and finally the
> cheapest sweet of all — black treacle. In the end sheer hunger, or my
> father's flat refusal to sell 'fancy relishes to them as can hardly buy
> bread and scran (margarine)', put a term to indulgence. (p. 110)

As the First World War approached, the residuum and those
fallen upon hard times were still dependent on bread to a
considerable extent and it is important not to underestimate that
proportion of the population who were still not benefiting from
the general improvement in working-class diets. Indeed, some
observers talk of a 'submerged third' in the period running up to
1914, and there is more than sufficient evidence to show the
hardships being endured by many millions of people. Nevertheless, the diets of the working classes in general had changed
beyond all recognition when compared to those of the 1850s and
1860s and this was reflected in the reduced importance of bread
purchases in the majority of household budgets. As war came,
family expenditure on food in the working class would have
been incomprehensibly lavish to the East London dockworker of
the 1860s.

The First World War brought great misery to many millions of
people yet at the same time, by 1918, the unskilled workmen

and their families were better fed than in 1913. Food shortages had first become serious in 1916, and people were asked to voluntarily restrict the amount of food they consumed. In 1917 King George V issued an 'Eat Less Bread' proclamation, and rationing was introduced on certain products. Bakers were compelled to bake 'Government bread', a compound of barley, rice, maize, beans and oatmeal, and in October 1917 they were allowed to add 1 lb of potatoes to 7 lbs of flour in the manufacturing process. In 1918, general civilian rationing was introduced although bread (now of minimal quality) was exempt. Whilst the system was certainly abused by the wealthier members of society, rations, however small, were always available at a price which the poorest could afford and offered a form of security to those in the greatest need. By the end of the war, food quality and quantity was low but survival was not in question for those living in poverty.

The interwar years began in the same vein. The general system of food rationing lasted until the end of November 1920 and what was to prove to be a short-lived industrial boom saw significant improvements in the overall living conditions of all groups. In 1921, however, a slump of massive proportions arrived, effectively destroying the postwar recovery within twelve months. The lowest-paid, unskilled workers saw an erosion of the advance in standards, which they had made in 1919 and 1920, but nevertheless living conditions were still well above those of 1914 (Branson 1975) and this improvement was maintained for most people through the middle years of the 1920s. The estimated annual consumption per head of bread, between 1924 and 1928, was only 94 per cent of that between 1909–13 but this reflected a better balanced diet in which substantially greater quantities of fruit, vegetables, butter and eggs were consumed (Orr 1936).

Again, these aggregate statistics disguise the fact that, for those most seriously hit by the 1921 slump — that is, those concentrated in the particularly depressed areas of Glasgow, Tyneside, Lancashire and South Wales — living conditions throughout the twenties were especially hard. Unemployment in these areas continued to rise that decade and, at the height of the crisis, in 1931, there were 3 million out of work, representing one in five of the labour force. The poverty of those in the 'special' areas stood in marked contrast to those in the Midlands and the South, where new light industries and consumer trades were much less affected (Burnett 1979).

The year 1931 was the turning point of the depression and conditions began to improve during the 1930s, although there were still over a million out of work when the Second World War broke out. Orr (1936) again found that the rate of increase in per-capita consumption between 1924–8 and 1934 was greater than in the previous fifteen years, and on his evidence the 1930s diet was better and cheaper than ever before. However, for the poorest group (10 per cent of the population or 4½ million people) diet was still deficient in every constituent examined, and this was confirmed by a 1936 study — carried out in York by Rowntree — which showed that virtually all families living on unemployment benefit and assistance were surviving on a diet which fell far below a 'human needs' standard.

In so far as bread consumption was concerned, Orr found that by 1934 it was almost uniform across the different income groups, although there were then great variations in the consumption of protein foods. Rowntree (1941) found that in 1936 for a poor, but typical family in York — comprising an unemployed man, his wife and four dependent children, and spending on average 16s. 10d. per week on food — expenditure on bread (made at home from flour and yeast) was only 13.8 per cent of the total food budget. A more prosperous family (man, wife and three children, with the man in work) spent only 8.5 per cent of their food budget (19s. 8½d.) on flour and yeast, while a plasterer, earning 72s. a week, supporting a wife and three children and buying rather than making bread, spent 33s. 8d. per week on food, of which approximately 8.6 per cent went on white and brown bread.

Rowntree's findings were confirmed by a comprehensive study carried out by Crawford and Broadley in 1936–7. They found that the poorest section of society — those earning less than £125 per annum — were spending some 12 per cent of the weekly food budget on bread whilst the most wealthy were spending only 3 per cent. However, variations around these figures are not hard to discover and they lend weight to the arguments of those who claim that such statistics served only to disguise the extremes of poverty in which people were living.

Orwell (1937) examined the expenditure on food of an unemployed Wigan miner, living in the heart of a depressed area. Here, expenditure on bread for the miner, his wife and two small children came to 23.7 per cent of the total food budget, and there can be little doubt that in the severely depressed regions many others were still spending 20–25 per cent of their weekly budget on bread. However, the evidence of Orr, Rowntree and Crawford and Broadley shows that, for the country as a whole, the majority of the poor were spending only 12–15 per cent of their food budget on bread — a statistic which shows a sharp decline over the 20–25 per cent figure to be found before the First World War.

Rowntree had estimated that the standard of living available to workers in 1936 was approximately 30 per cent higher than it had been in 1899. Certainly, by 1939, the dominant position of bread in the majority of working-class family diets had disappeared, and the paradox, which Giffen had observed among the poorer labouring classes of the mid-nineteenth century, was impossible to find among their great-grandchildren.

* * *

The appearance, in 1895, of Marshall's reference to the paradox came at a time when the living standards of the working class were substantially improving. As the twentieth century began, the dominance of bread in the diets of the poor was beginning to decline and the conditions necessary to produce the paradox were more difficult to find. In the years after 1900, therefore, it was inevitable that the paradox would be seen as increasingly esoteric and theoretical.

Marshall's statement in 1895 had nevertheless been quickly followed by another from an equally authoritative source. In the second volume of his *Cours d'Economie Politique*, published in 1897, Vilfredo Pareto had also stated the paradox:

> L'augmentation du prix d'une marchandise qui n'a pas de succédanés a pour effet immédiat d'en restreindre la consommation. L'augmentation du prix d'une marchandise qui a des succédanés peut, au contraire, avoir pour premier effet d'augmenter la consommation.

Pour nous rendre compte de cet effet, en apparence paradoxal, considérons un exemple. L'alimentation constitue le principal chapitre du budget des classes pauvres. Supposons que des individus de ces classes se nourrissent de viande, de pain et de pommes de terre. Le pain vient à augmenter de prix. Les individus considérés tâcheront de réduire les dépenses en dehors de l'aliment-ation, mais ils n'épargneront ainsi que fort peu de chose. La réduction devra s'étendre à l'alimentation elle-même, et ils devront renoncer à l'usage de la viande. Mais, par la même, ils se trouveront dans la nécessité de manger une plus grande quantité de pain. Le premier effet d'une hausse du prix aura donc été de faire augmenter la demande de pain. Si la hausse continue, les individus considérés devront faire de nouveaux sacrifices. Après avoir renoncé à l'usage de la viande, pour se nourrir de pain, ils devront encore substituer au pain les pommes de terre. Alors, la consommation diminuera. (Cours II, p. 338)

Pareto, like Marshall, did not support this statement of the paradox with any specific evidence, and it was this lack of proof which was again controversial. In his letter to Edgeworth, in 1909, defending Rea's views on the perverse demand for wheat (Pigou 1925), Marshall was at a loss to supply any evidence for the paradox beyond noting that he had compared the amount of bread eaten by the rich, the middle class and the poor and that he 'was convinced that the rich eat less than half as much bread as the poorer classes: the middle class coming midway'. This observation, of course, had little to do with the Giffen paradox and not surprisingly drew no response from Edgeworth. In a letter written to Edgeworth the next day, however, Marshall referred to those parts of his 1903 Memorandum on the Fiscal Policy of International Trade which dealt with wheat supply and took up a similar theme. This time he came nearer to the matter:

I am even more perplexed by what you say about elasticity of demand. . . . I object to the phrase negative elasticity, because I think it tempts people to carry analytical mathematics beyond their proper scope. In this case, for instance, it suggests a paradox. And I submit that there is no paradox at all. Take a parallel case. I believe that people in Holland travel by canal boat instead of railway sometimes on account of its cheapness. Suppose a man was in a hurry to make a journey of 150 kilos. He had two florins for it and no more. The fare by boat was one cent a kilo, by third class train two cents. So he decided to go 100 kilos by boat and fifty by train: total cost two florins. On arriving at the boat he found the charge had been raised to 1¼ cents per kilo. 'Oh: then I will travel 133⅓ kilos (or as near as may be) by boat, I can't afford more than 16⅔ kilos by train'. Why not? Where is the paradox? (Pigou 1925, p. 441)

Here, substitution of bread and meat for boat and train shows an argument much closer to the paradox, although the discussion is centred on Giffen-like goods and Giffenesque behaviour rather than on the original Giffen paradox. It is interesting to note, however, that Marshall denied that such behaviour was in any way paradoxical. Indeed, Marshall never claimed that Giffen himself had observed and reported an economic paradox.

Marshall's only two attempts to provide substance for his reference to Giffen in *Principles* are unconvincing, and his arguments concerning the consumption of bread in hotels and Dutch travel show how he himself appeared to be ill at ease with the subject. However, his problems are to some extent understandable. By 1909 empirical evidence of the paradox would have been hard to find as bread expenditure as a percentage of the total household food budget was falling significantly and had nothing in common with the much higher percentages which had been observed in the 1850s and 1860s. Marshall therefore, was still defending the paradox in 1909 but added little of substance to the debate. Edgeworth, meanwhile, remained unconvinced both of the credentials and of the significance of the phenomenon. This view, however, was to be modified in later years.

Whilst no detailed search for empirical evidence of the paradox was undertaken in the years immediately after 1910, research into related areas continued. First, Engel's consumption theories relating to the demand for food were taken further. Gini (1910) claimed that arithmetic increases in food consumption implied geometric decreases in food prices, and vice versa, while del Vecchio (1912) argued that although increases or decreases in income are geometric, percentages of income spent on food move arithmetically in the opposite direction.

Soon afterwards, another positively-sloped demand curve suggested by the paradox was being 'discovered'. Moore (1914) believed he had identified 'a new type of demand curve' on the basis of his research into the demand for pig iron in the United States over the years 1870–1911. He claimed to have found that demand for what he termed 'our representative producer's good' (the industrial equivalent of bread?) had been higher during a period of rising prices (1890–1911) than during a period of falling prices (1866–90):

> . . . if we assume that all demand curves are of the same negative type, we are confronted with an impossibility at the very beginning of our investigation. Upon the assumption that all demand curves are of the negative type, it would be impossible for general prices to fall while the yield per acre of crops is decreasing. In consequence of the decrease in the yield per acre, the price of crops would ascend, the volume of commodities represented by pig-iron would decrease, and upon the hypothesis of the universality of the descending type of demand curves, the prices of commodities like pig-iron would rise. In a period of declining yield of crops, therefore, there would be a rise of prices. . . . But the facts are exactly the contrary. (2, p. 112)

Moore argued that he had, in fact, found a positively sloping demand curve for a basic industrial commodity. His claim, however, brought a quick response. Lehfeldt (1915) wrote:

> The author thinks he has discovered a new type of demand curve, sloping the opposite way to the usual kind. But the curve (for pig-iron) . . . is not a demand curve at all, but much more nearly a supply curve. It is arrived at by the intersection of irregularly fluctuating demands on supply conditions, that, on the whole, may be regarded as steady except for a secular growth, whereas the whole line of argument with regard to crops is based on considering the intersection of irregular supply (due to fluctuations of weather) with a steady demand. (p. 411)

Lehfeldt's rejection of Moore's claim was later supported by Fanno (1916), and Moore did not choose to dispute the fact that he had confused demand with supply curves. Indeed, by 1923, the positively sloping demand curve had been replaced by the 'law of competitive price' which stated that manufacturers' costs of production increase as agricultural and mining products themselves increase in price — a singularly unremarkable law.

At the same time that Gini and del Vecchio were adding to income and expenditure theory and Moore was (briefly) discovering an upward sloping demand curve, mathematical economists were addressing the Giffen paradox more directly. Johnson (1913), in discussing the pure theory of utility curves, described the paradox in mathematical terms, showing that, exceptionally, the quantity purchased of a commodity could well increase with a rise in its price. Similarly, Zawadski (1914) complained that constancy of the marginal value of money had been too freely taken for granted by economists — Marshall, in particular — in developing theories of value and utility.

In so far as the paradox itself was concerned, Zawadski wrote:

> What is the value of such a conclusion? Is it not in flagrant contradiction with the facts? It is easy to imagine theoretical cases in which the demand should decrease upon a diminution in the price. Theory should, therefore, be able to give an account of them. Do they actually occur (and under the statistical hypothesis) otherwise than by way of exception? What may be their importance? Here are some questions and one might ask several others to which theory does not provide us with answers. In this example we put our fingers as it were, on the strength and the weakness of mathematical economics. We have a most general formula which embraces even the extremely rare cases, but we are not able to pass on to the particular cases or even to distinguish the exception to the rule. (p. 186)

From this, it is clear that Zawadski was either unaware of the Giffen example, which had been quoted by Marshall nearly twenty years earlier, or had given the Giffen case no credence. Certainly Edgeworth (1915) remained unconvinced of the significance of such perverse demand, arguing that Marshall had assigned to the doctrine 'just the amount of space which is due to it in a treatise [*Principles*] not primarily concerned with mathematical abstractions'. However, he did acknowledge for the first time that the paradox could occur:

> Thus it is recorded of a local dearth that, the price of bread rising very high, the price of meat and other articles fell off, owing to the fact that the purchasers of those articles had to expend so much of their money on bread. In this instance, presumably, the less necessary articles followed the law of 'short periods' ('market value'); the dealers sold their goods below cost price. Otherwise we might suppose the prices of articles other than bread — including that of meat — to be kept constant. Under these conditions . . . it is conceivable that more bread might be purchased. But this occurrence is probably attended with a rise in the marginal utility of money. (p. 61)

Whilst Marshall, therefore, had certainly not been able to satisfy Edgeworth with specific evidence for the paradox, by 1915 Edgeworth was prepared to concede the theoretical point. In 1925 he went further by including in his *Papers Relating to Political Economy* a section on paradoxes, one of which was indexed as 'a rise of price attended with increase of consumption'. Again, he made reference to Johnson and Zawadski and, while arguing that for the great majority of purchases, common sense was 'violently contrary' to such manifestations of perverse demand, he was prepared to admit to the special case when the product in question was a major item in an individual's total expenditure and when the price increase was substantial enough to affect the marginal utility of money to that individual. Quoting Professor Carver (1896) who had claimed 'It is scarcely conceivable that a tax can increase the demand for the thing taxed', Edgeworth notes 'Yet we have seen that this hardly conceivable, is not impossible' (p. 479).

By 1925, therefore, Edgeworth, who some 16 years earlier had rejected the paradox as both incredible and unfounded, was a convert to the view that, under certain exceptional circumstances, price changes could affect the marginal utility of money to such an extent that an economic paradox could occur. However, he treated the subject very much as a mathematical economist, accepting the logic of the 'curiosum' which had been independently identified by Johnson and by Zawadski (after Pareto). At the same time, he remained convinced that it was no more than a curiosum, arguing that 'the proposition should rather be referred to the chapter of tentatives, if it can be supposed to have a bearing on practice'. Unlike Marshall, Edgeworth had treated such exceptional behaviour as a paradox, but at no time did he make reference to Giffen as a past observer of such a phenomenon. Again, this is consistent with his view that, whilst it made an interesting if obscure mathematical point, it had little if any justification in terms of actual market behaviour. For Edgeworth, empirical evidence did not exist, and any reference to Giffen would have been superfluous.

Apart from the limited interest shown in the mathematics of the paradox, it was clearly being treated very much as a curiosum. Economic theories of demand which were at this time being developed and refined gave no recognition of this 'special case'. As early as 1910, Pigou — who in 1908 had written to Rea confirming that, in his opinion, demand for wheat in England had once been 'Giffen' — developed his theory of additive preferences: a theory which, as Deaton (1974) pointed out, made no concession to the possibility of paradox behaviour. Some fifteen years later, in 1925, Palgrave's *Dictionary of Political Economy* attributed the paradox statement to Simon Gray but referred to it as an example of his 'radical fallacies'. And a search through the new textbooks on economics reviewed in the *Economic Journal* between 1910 and 1940 produces hardly a reference to Giffen or to the paradox.

It was only towards the end of the 1930s that the paradox was once again being noticed. In 1934 Hicks and Allen had defended the concept of a 'rising' demand curve:

> This possibility can easily be recognised as the celebrated Giffen case referred to by Marshall when the consumption of bread may actually be reduced by a fall in its price. Our analysis shows that it is perfectly consistent with the principle of increasing marginal rate of substitution; but it is only possible at low levels of income, when a large proportion of expenditure is devoted to this 'inferior' commodity, and when, among the small number of other objects consumed, there are none that are at all easily substitutable for the first. As the standard of living rises, and expenditure becomes increasingly diversified it is a situation which becomes increasingly improbable. (pp. 68–9)

In 1937 Meyers identified the paradox as a rare exception to the downward-sloping demand curve, referring again to Marshall's comment in *Principles*. Schultz (1938) attributed the paradox not only to Giffen (through Marshall) but again to Simon Gray, and noted that the phenomenon was not consistent with the principle of diminishing utility. However, he thought it to be of limited value:

> The problem of a positively sloping demand curve may arise in statistical work when an attempt is made to deduce the demand for a commodity on the part of the very poor, from budget statistics giving quantities, prices and income. When, however, the demand relates to the entire country, the existence of such a function is extremely improbable. . . . In any event, the difficulties associated with the time variable in the statistical study of demand are so serious as to overshadow the extremely small probability that a commodity which

is consumed by rich and poor alike has a positively sloping demand curve. The statistical economist will be justified, therefore, in assuming that, when his data relate to a large market in which the demand of the very poor is incorporated with that of others, the quantity taken must decrease as price increases, when the disturbing factors are held constant, and that, when his statistical results contradict this assumption, there is something wrong with his analysis. (p. 51)

Giffen himself would have agreed with Schultz that aggregate data can conceal information on how market sectors actually behave. Nevertheless, Schultz was clearly not convinced that the paradox merited special attention and in this was only reflecting the views of the economic establishment through the 1920s and 1930s.

* * *

The interwar years had quite simply seen little interest in the paradox. Those few who had shown interest, moreover, believed that whilst it was an esoteric mathematical curiosum it had little, if any, practical significance. This view would certainly have been reinforced by the fact that by the 1920s and 1930s, as the earlier part of this chapter has shown, the conditions under which paradox behaviour could be observed were becoming increasingly rare — indeed, by 1939 they no longer existed in Britain for all practical purposes. Furthermore, throughout this period the credibility of the paradox was never measured against the living conditions of the poor in nineteenth-century Britain, when it was not at all uncommon to find people living largely on bread as their single staple food.

In these circumstances, lack of interest in the paradox as anything other than a theoretical nicety can be easily understood. Moreover, on the few occasions when the paradox was acknowledged and discussed at this time, it was generally not associated with Robert Giffen. The mathematical economists who had been developing demand theory after 1910 made no reference to him when discussing this special case, and a stronger association with Giffen only occurs in the 1930s when Marshall's theories of utility and value were once again coming under closer scrutiny by Hicks and others. Throughout the period, the paradox appeared either as a mathematical abstraction of little importance or as the exceptional 'Giffen case' quoted by Alfred Marshall in developing his theories of demand. At no time were the claims made for the paradox tested empirically or subject to more detailed examination, and there were no signs at all of any emerging interest.

In December 1942, the *Economic Journal* published a set of articles to commemorate the centenary of the birth of Alfred Marshall. Two Cambridge University papers — on the evolution of Marshall's *Principles of Economics* (Guillebaud) and on the place of *Principles* in economic theory (Shove) — looked in some detail at his most famous work. In neither paper, however, was any mention made of the paradox or of its claim to be the significant exception to Marshall's law of demand. Any concern with Giffen's special case seemed to be disappearing, but the later 1940s were to see the start of a far greater interest in the phenomenon and in its implications for demand theory.

References

Ashton, T.S. (1948) *The Industrial Revolution, 1760–1830,* Oxford University Press.

Beeke, H. (1800) 'Memorial on the dearness of corn', *Sidmouth Papers,* Devon P.R.O. 152/M/C1800/0G4.

Booth, C. (1889) *Life and Labour of the People in London.* First Series: *Poverty,* Vol. 1: East, Central and South London, Williams & Norgate.

Booth, W. (1890) *In Darkest England and the Way Out,* Salvation Army.

Bowley, A.L. (1895) 'Changes in average wages (nominal and real) in the United Kingdom between 1860 and 1891', *Journal of the Royal Statistical Society,* Vol. 58, p. 225.

Branson, N. (1975) *Britain in the Nineteen Twenties,* Weidenfeld & Nicolson.

Burnett, J. (1979) *Plenty and Want,* Scolar Press, (first published by Nelson 1966).

Carver, T.N. (1896) 'The shifting of taxes', *Yale Review* (November), pp. 258–71.

Crawford, W. and Broadley, H. (1938) *The People's Food,* Heinemann.

Davenant, C. (1699) 'An essay upon the probable methods of making a people gainers in the balance of trade'. Davenant's 'law' — that 'a defect in the harvest raises the price of corn in calculable proportions' — is commonly attributed to Gregory King.

Davies, D. (1795) *The Case of Labourers in Husbandry*.
Deaton, A. (1974) 'A reconsideration of the empirical implications of additive preferences', *Economic Journal*, Vol. 84, pp. 338–48.
del Vecchio, G. (1912) 'Relazioni fra entrata e consumo', *Giornale degli economisti*, Vol. 44, pp. 111–42, 228–54, 389–439.
Ducpetiaux, E. (1855) *Budgets économiques des classes ouvrières en Belgique*.
Eden, F. (1797) *The State of the Poor*.
Edgeworth, F.W. (1915) 'Recent contributions to mathematical economics', *Economic Journal*, Vol. 25, pp. 36–63, 189–203.
Edgeworth, F.W. (1925) *Papers Relating to Political Economy*, Macmillan.
Engel, E. (1857) 'Die Produktions- und Consumtionsverhältnisse des Königreichs Sachsen', reprinted as an appendix to *Die Lebenskosten belgischer Arbeiter-Familien* (1895).
Fanno, M. (1916), 'Review of *Economic Cycles*', *Giornale degli economisti*, Vol. 52, pp. 151–4.
Gini, C. (1910) 'Prezzi e consumi', *Giornale degli economisti*, Vol. 40, pp. 99–114, 235–49.
Gray, S. (1815) *The Happiness of States: Or an Inquiry Concerning Population, the Modes of Subsisting and Employing It, and the Effects of All on Human Happiness*, Hatchard.
Guillebaud, C.W. (1942) 'The Evolution of Marshall's *Principles of Economics*', *Economic Journal*, Vol. 52 (December), pp. 330–49.
Higgs, H. (ed.) (1925) *Palgrave's Dictionary of Political Economy*, Vol. 1, Macmillan.
Hicks, J.R. and Allen, R.G.D. (1934) 'A reconsideration of the theory of value — part 1', *Economica* (February), pp. 52–76.
Johnson, W.E. (1913) 'The pure theory of utility curves', *Economic Journal*, Vol. 23, pp. 483–513.
Koenker, R. (1977) 'Was bread Giffen? The demand for food in England circa 1790', *Review of Economics and Statistics*, Vol. 59 (May), pp. 225–9.
Lehfeldt, R.A. (1915) 'Review of *Economic Cycles*', *Economic Journal*, Vol. 25, pp. 409–11.
Marshall, A. (1895) *Principles of Economics* (3rd edn), Macmillan.
Marshall, A. (1903) 'Memorandum on the fiscal policy of international trade'. The essay was first written in 1903 and revised for publication in 1909. It appears in J. Keynes (ed.) (1926) *Official Papers by Alfred Marshall*, Macmillan.
Meyers, A.L. (1937) *Elements of Modern Economics*, Prentice-Hall.
Moore, H.L. (1914) *Economic Cycles: Their Law and Cause*, Macmillan.
Orr, J.B. (1936) *Food, Health and Income. Report on a Survey of Adequacy of Diet in Relation to Income*.
Orwell, G. (1937) *The Road to Wigan Pier*, Gollancz.
Pareto, V. (1897) *Le Cours d'Economie Politique*, Vol. 2, Librairie de l'Université, Lausanne.
Pigou, A.C. (1910) 'A method of determining the numerical value of elasticities of demand', *Economic Journal*, Vol. 20, pp. 636–40.
Pigou, A.C. (ed.) (1925) *Memorials of Alfred Marshall*, Macmillan.

Rashid, S. (1979) 'The Beeke good: a note on the origins of the "Giffen good"', *History of Political Economy*, Vol. 11, No. 4, pp. 606–7.

Roberts, R. (1971) *The Classic Slum*, Manchester University Press.

Rowntree, B. Seebohm (1901) *Poverty: A Study of Town Life*, Macmillan.

Rowntree, B. Seebohm (1941) *Poverty and Progress; A Second Social Survey of York*, Longman.

Russell, C.E.B. (1905) *Manchester Boys*, Sherratt & Hughes.

Schultz, H. (1938) *The Theory and Measurement of Demand*, Chicago University Press.

Shove, G.F. (1942) 'The place of Marshall's *Principles* in the development of economic theory', *Economic Journal*, Vol. 52 (December), pp. 294–329.

Zawadski, W. (1914) *Les Mathématiques Appliquées à l'Économie Politique*, Rivière.

* * *

Factories Inquiry (1833), Royal Commission First Report, Section D1, pp. 39–40.

First Annual Report of the Poor Law Commissioners for England and Wales (1835), p. 187.

Memoranda, Statistical Tables and Charts prepared in the Board of Trade with reference to various matters bearing on British and Foreign Trade and Industrial Conditions, Cd. 1761 (1903), 2nd Series, Cd. 2337 (1904).

CHAPTER 8

Rehabilitation and Debate

By the time of the Second World War, the conditions which produced paradox behaviour could no longer be found in Britain. As the military crisis deepened, the Government moved quickly to control food prices and to ration essential items in order to ensure the equitable distribution and availability of food. In 1940 Bowley, reviewing an Oxford University Institute of Statistics survey of wartime working-class budgets, commented that 'in brief, there are indications that the demand for "circuses" is more urgent than that for "bread"'. After the war, bread was in fact rationed between July 1946 and July 1948, and 1947–8 saw dietary conditions deteriorate relative to 1945. Nevertheless, even in 1947–8 diet was substantially better than the average prewar diet in almost all nutrients and by the early 1950s it was better in every respect.

Over the one hundred years since 1860, the diet of the British working class had in fact improved most dramatically following two particular periods of crisis — the Great Depression of the 1880s and the wartime and immediate postwar years of the 1940s. The improvements, however, had been brought about for different reasons:

> In both cases the basic reason for improvement was the same — a rising standard of living resulting from an increase in the purchasing power of the population. But here the parallel ends. In the first period this increased spending power was due to external factors over which the Government exercised no control — the emergence of great primary producing countries and developments in communications and technology which made possible the mass importation of cheap food; in the second, the State took a direct part by fixing prices, by rationing and by deliberately pursuing a nutritional and social policy which succeeded in raising standards at a time of acute national peril. (Burnett 1979, p. 322)

The effect of these two decades, together with the steady, if less spectacular progress achieved over the fifty years which separated them, was to effectively remove the conditions under which the Giffen paradox could occur in Britain. Moreover, the substantial improvement in diet was to continue through the 1950s and 1960s. Between 1950 and 1976, according to the National Food Survey statistics, the weekly consumption of white bread per head in Britain halved (from 50.91 oz. to 26.43 oz.): a sign of the increasing affluence which had seen the replacement of cheap energy foods in the diet with more expensive protein sources. By 1976 expenditure on bread (white and brown) represented only 6.2 per cent of total weekly expenditure on food.

Although the continued improvements in diet and the increasing affluence of the population after 1945 could have been expected to remove any residual curiosity about the paradox, this was not, in fact, the case. On the contrary, interest in the special Giffen phenomenon and in its origins was heightened when Stigler became the first academic to look closely at the origins of the paradox and to publish his findings in 1947. This paper, and the subsequent debate with Prest (1948) (see Chapter 2), served to renew interest in a subject which had up to that time received little serious attention.

Stigler's own interest in the paradox must itself have been stimulated by a slightly earlier event. In the May 1945 edition of the *Journal of Farm Economics*, he had presented a study of the costs and quantities of basic foodstuffs which were considered part of the adequate yearly diet for Americans in the years 1939 and 1944. Having analysed data for the two years in question he observed: 'In this connection it is interesting to notice that the quantity of wheat flour is increased substantially between the two dates, although its price rose more than other eligible cereals. This is an artificial example of the Giffen Paradox. . . .' (p. 312).

Stigler's claim to have found a modern if artificial example of the paradox caused Samuelson (1946) to point out that Stigler had not in fact identified an example of paradox behaviour because substitution rather than income effects explained the case in question. This confusion over the exact meaning of the Giffen paradox would certainly have aroused Stigler's curiosity about the phenomenon and made him aware of how little was actually known about this exception to the law of demand.

The research carried out by Stigler and Prest in 1947–8 — the only work of any substance relating to the origins of the paradox and their exchange — did not succeed in generating any great interest in a special case which had been largely neglected for some fifty years. However, although no further research was carried out either into its history or into the empirical evidence of such behaviour, the paradox attracted attention again one year later for entirely different reasons.

In 1949 Milton Friedman proposed an alternative interpretation of Marshall's demand curve, arguing that the phrase 'other things the same', usually associated with the definition of the law of demand, gave rise to misinterpretation. Instead of taking 'other things' to refer to the tastes and preferences of purchasers, their *money* income and the price of every other commodity, Friedman proposed an alternative: the tastes and preferences of purchasers, their *real* income and the price of every closely-related commodity. The case for real income to be held constant rested on the proposition that a higher price for any commodity would trigger compensating changes in the prices of other goods.

In arguing for his new interpretation of Marshall, Friedman could find only one passage in the text of *Principles* which was inconsistent with his new approach — the 'celebrated passage . . . which deals with the so-called "Giffen phenomenon"'. However, he felt able to reconcile this exception with his new theory, arguing that it was a rare case associated with a small, atypical group:

> This passage clearly offsets an income effect against a substitution effect, whereas, on my interpretation of Marshall, real income is the same at all points on the demand, so there is no 'income effect'. . . . The passage is thus in the spirit of the current interpretation. Yet the words I have italicized ('poorer labouring families' in Marshall's paragraph on the paradox) indicate that it does not necessarily contradict my interpretation of Marshall. The purchasing power of money and the real income of the community at large may remain constant; yet the real income of a particular group in the community that has a special consumption pattern may be adversely affected by the rise in the price of a particular commodity. (p. 486)

Nonetheless, Friedman had to concede that, even under his new interpretation of the law of demand, the Giffen paradox remained a special case which stood outside general theory — special in the sense that the dependence of a particular social group on a single staple commodity could be so great that, even allowing for some compensating movement in other prices, the income effect of a price rise of that staple commodity would be significant in real income as well as in money income terms.

Once again, discussion of the paradox had taken place in a theoretical context and this was to continue. In 1950 Stigler, reviewing the development of utility theory, again made reference to the paradox. In acknowledging that Pareto (1897) and Johnson (1913) had joined Marshall in accepting the possibility of positively-sloping demand curves under exceptional circumstances, he nevertheless argued that preoccupation with such esoteric niceties 'marks a fruitless digression from the viewpoint of the progress of utility theory'. However, he went further (p. 395), referring to the inability of casual knowledge to 'reject even the imaginary Giffen paradox'.

Stigler's views, therefore, seem to have undergone a substantial change between 1945, when he claimed to have seen recent evidence of the paradox in the United States, and 1950, when he saw it as an altogether 'imaginary' phenomenon. It is not clear why this reassessment came about but it must be assumed that Stigler's investigations into the paradox in 1947 had not only proved fruitless but had also persuaded him that there had never been any evidence for such exceptional consumer behaviour and that the phenomenon had no basis in fact.

In 1956 Alford looked again at the paradox in the context of Marshall's demand curve and argued that, far from being imaginary, it had been included in the third edition of *Principles* 'due to a change in the factual material available to Marshall' (p. 42). He also pointed out that elsewhere in *Principles* wheat had been used to illustrate an exception to the general law of the variation in demand elasticity but that there had strangely been no cross-reference between this and the Giffen case which provided a much more striking exception to this law. Alford did not suggest what additional factual information had been made available to Marshall in 1895 but Gramm (1970) implied that Prest had been correct and that it had appeared in Giffen's evidence to the Royal Commission on Agricultural Depression. Prest's 'discovery' had however been challenged by Stigler as having produced no clear statement of a consumption paradox.

Like Alford, Gramm was unhappy with Friedman's alternative interpretation of Marshall's demand curve. In particular, he claimed that Marshall's general methodological approach had been misunderstood and that the 'constant purchasing power' assumption had been made by Marshall for theoretical reasoning but not on an empirical basis:

> In general, Marshall developed tools to deal with actual market situations. In most practical problems the income effect is of the 'second order of small quantities' and his theoretical formulation of the demand curve is directly applicable to actual market situations. Only in the extreme case, Giffen's Paradox, is the income effect present in a perceivable magnitude and thus warrants formal recognition as an exception to the general case where Marshall's formulation was a workable approximation of reality. (p. 68)

Gramm also recognised that the paradox statement was usually taken out of context and was in reality part of a larger section which had been added to the third edition of *Principles* to acknowledge the fact that there were some (very rare) occasions when the purchasing power of money needed to be taken into account in analysing price–demand relationships. Chapter 5 has demonstrated that this insert had in fact been made necessary by the debate concerning the marginal utility of income with which Professors Nicholson, Edgeworth and Marshall had become very much involved and which had driven Marshall to make some concessions with regard to exceptional consumer behaviour. The existence of Giffen's paradox had, in fact, taken Marshall beyond the boundaries of his theoretical model and such behaviour had had to be acknowledged as the exception which served to prove the general rule rather than to undermine his theory of demand.

Gramm's paper offered a constructive analysis of the place of the Giffen paradox in Marshallian theory, but by 1970 it was clear that discussion of the phenomenon was, for the most part, becoming sterile and circular. In the absence of any empirical work to add a fresh perspective to the debate, there seemed little possibility of moving forward. However, in 1971 a new dimension was added — again, it came not from empirical advances but from a reformulation of theory.

In 1966 Lancaster had published his paper on consumer theory in which he argued that, for the purposes of demand analysis, goods were better seen as sets of 'characteristics' which, separately and together, generated varying levels of consumer interest and demand. Lancaster's reformulation of the theory of consumer choice provided a model which was capable of allowing for some reconsideration of the paradox, and in 1971 Lipsey and Rosenbluth published a paper on this theme, using both Hicks (1956) and Lancaster (1966) as their theoretical bases.

Lipsey and Rosenbluth focused not on the original Giffen paradox — that is, not specifically on the demand for bread on the part of the poor — but on the nature of so-called 'Giffen goods', and on the extent to which a 'Giffen effect' could be expected to occur in modern society. They were critical of the treatment of these effects both by adherents of more traditional demand theory (in particular of Hicksian indifference theory and of the 'revealed preference' approach of Samuelson) and by proponents of the new theory of consumer demand which had been put forward by Lancaster. Both Hicks and Lancaster had argued that the Giffen effect was an unlikely event which had seldom if ever been found in practice. However, Lipsey and Rosenbluth claimed that, as Marshall himself had illustrated by his reference to Dutch transportation in his 1909 letter to Edgeworth (see Chapter 7), Giffen effects were in no sense paradoxical and were far more commonplace than both traditional and modern theorists had acknowledged.

The 1971 paper argued that while bread and meat, beer and whisky and Marshall's transport example had been most commonly used to illustrate the existence of Giffen goods and the Giffen effect, in reality, and particularly when Lancaster's view of goods as having sets of 'characteristics' was accepted, many purchasing decisions were capable of producing similar effects in the market. Giffen goods could exist, Lipsey and Rosenbluth claimed, not only as a result of poverty but also because of the satiation of certain characteristics of goods in richer societies. They then proceeded to redefine a Giffen good:

1. It may have only one characteristic or it may have more.

2. There must be at least one 'superior' good that shares at least one of its characteristics with the Giffen good. If the shared characteristic is not satiated, the superior good must have another characteristic with a relatively high income elasticity of demand. This characteristic must be either not produced at all by the Giffen good or else produced by it at a comparative disadvantage to the superior good.

3. A Giffen good can have an absolute advantage in all of the characteristics that it produces in common with other goods, provided that the characteristic in which it has a comparative advantage is a satiable one. In this case the Giffen phenomenon will occur at a high enough level of income so that consumption of the satiable characteristic is actually in the range of satiation. Thus we need not think only of wheat in the diet of nineteenth-century British farm labourers but also of beer in the diet of twentieth-century American city dwellers when we look for examples of possible Giffen goods.

4. A good will necessarily be Giffen over some parts of the price range that give rise to positive imputed prices of all relevant characteristics if it has a comparative advantage *either* in producing a characteristic that is only useful if consumed in multiples of some fixed finite amount, *or* in producing a characteristic that is 'absolutely satiable'. (p. 147)

Lipsey and Rosenbluth, therefore, proposed a radical new definition of those goods which were and those which were not capable of being Giffen, and of the circumstances which could, in fact, produce the Giffen effect. Whilst accepting that inferiority was a necessary, but insufficient condition for a good to be 'Giffen' when goods were distinguished from 'characteristics', they rejected the argument that it had to have a high proportion of income spent on it. Overall, they argued that the rarity of the Giffen effect had not been established at the theoretical level. In so far as empirical evidence was concerned, they rejected Stigler's view that there was an almost total absence of exceptions to the law of demand, and claimed that in a review of some thirty papers and monographs on demand measurement, published between 1960 and 1970, 'the frequency with which positive price coefficients are found leads us to believe that the existing empirical evidence does not support Stigler's contention' (p. 159).

The importance of the Lipsey and Rosenbluth paper lay in its attempt to shift the focus of discussion away from the nineteenth-century Giffen paradox and towards the proposition that in any situation where one good has a comparative advantage in a satiated characteristic a Giffen effect can occur, and at any level of income. Marshall had, indeed, identified such Giffen-like effects when, in 1909, he used the example of consumer choice between two competing means of transportation within a given travel budget and in circumstances where one mode of transport (canal boat) was clearly inferior to the other (rail) in terms of time costs. Lipsey and Rosenbluth, building on this and similar examples, attempted to demonstrate the relative frequency with which Giffenesque behaviour could occur, both in theoretical and in practical terms, and argued that Giffen goods would have to be defined far more generously in the future, to allow for the possibility of satiated characteristics among competing goods, and for the seemingly perverse price–demand consequences that can arise.

After 1971, other writers followed Lipsey and Rosenbluth in arguing for a new, wider interpretation of the Giffen phenomenon. Vandermeulen (1972), in a paper written without reference to the Lipsey and Rosenbluth work, went further: 'The Giffen case must be purged of what is, unfortunately, its most persuasive feature, any implication that devoting a high percentage of an abnormally low real income to a single commodity influences a consumer's preferences . . . the Giffen case, far from being necessary, actually represents the set of conditions least likely to generate an upward sloping demand curve' (p. 453). He attempted to demonstrate that a high percentage of income spent on a commodity was in no sense a necessary or even a predisposing condition for a positively-sloped demand curve and that the share of income was irrelevant. He also argued that abnormally low real incomes actually tended to prevent upward-sloping demand schedules, and concluded: 'Thus, the virtual identification of a positive price effect with the Giffen case has served economists badly. It has directed attention toward the least likely of empirical conditions and has given false assurance of the near infallibility of the law of demand' (p. 458).

Clearly, Vandermeulen's view was more radical than that of Lipsey and Rosenbluth; but others were to argue that Giffen goods were more common than had been supposed. Steindl (1973) suggested that under certain conditions money and bonds must be seen as Giffen goods. In so far as money was concerned, an increase in its price, relative to the price of bonds (i.e. an increase in the interest rate), could, he claimed, result in an increase in the amount of money demanded. Changes in the prices of consols were held to produce similar effects, and when the analysis was extended to the more realistic, three assets case, capital could also be seen as a Giffen good.

Bopp (1983) claimed that Giffen-like behaviour was linked to the demand for a more mundane commodity. Looking at movements in the price of kerosene in the United States — a product which has a close substitute (fuel oil), and which has the potential to consume a large part of a low-income budget when kerosene furnaces are used to burn a mixture of kerosene and regular heating fuels — Bopp found that, over the years 1967–76, a rise in the price of kerosene had reduced real incomes significantly enough to ensure that purchases of other fuels, used in the mix with kerosene, were cut back and that more kerosene was purchased to run furnaces in smaller homes.

Steindl and Bopp had produced data which, they claimed, illustrated Giffenesque behaviour in line with the Lipsey and Rosenbluth thesis, but both studies were, in part, unconvincing. Steindl did not acknowledge some normal substitution effects at work in the management of his two-good and three-good profit-maximising portfolio, while Bopp had to recognise that kerosene was not, in fact, cheaper but more expensive than the regular fuel oils used in the furnace mixtures. However, both papers did illustrate the seeming ease with which something close to paradox behaviour could be observed in different market situations. In the wake of the Lipsey and Rosenbluth paper, the term 'Giffen good' was without question being more liberally redefined to include many categories of product other than staple foodstuffs.

At the same time, a more traditional debate concerning the 'old' paradox had continued. De Alessi (1968) explored its testability in terms of the possible falseness of conventional demand theory but concluded that, without hard evidence, negatively sloped demand curves had to be accepted. Mayston (1976) argued that the paradox, in any event, was not at odds with Marshall's demand theory, once it was recognised that levels of welfare change along Marshallian individual demand curves and that Marshall himself did not assume that utilities were additive. Boland (1977), unhappy with the theory under-pinning the work of Lipsey and Rosenbluth, argued that it was self-contradictory and capable of rendering standard price theory untestable, or worse, irrelevant (p. 73). Furthermore, he argued that they had not disposed of the Hicks case (that the Giffen paradox was an extremely rare event) as comprehensively as they had imagined:

> [They] argue that Giffen goods are more likely when we base utility on 'characteristics' rather than the goods themselves. Unfortunately, they use Lancaster's linear model of the relationship between goods and characteristics and it is the linearity alone which produces their result. There are many possible non-linear models of characteristics production which would yield the Hicksian conclusions concerning 'likelihood'. (p. 81n)

Boland claimed that Giffen goods and market-determined prices were incompatible and that, in any event, demand theory was concerned with explaining quantities demanded which, in turn, explain price equilibrium. His conclusion was that Giffen-like behaviour could occur at the level of the individual but could not determine aggregate demand curves concerned with overall markets and market-clearing prices.

Giffen himself would not have opposed the view that the paradox related not to overall market demand for a commodity but to the demand generated by a particular group of indivi-duals facing exceptional income constraints. At the theoretical level, however, Dougan (1982) argued that Boland's interpre-tation was wrong in that: 'Marshallian stability is an inappro-priate condition in the Giffen case for the reason that by the very nature of a Giffen good's demand curve there is no unique "demand price" for certain quantities. It is therefore unnecessary to rule out Giffen market demand curves as a condition of equilibrium. . . .' (p. 815n). Dougan was more sympathetic to the Lipsey and Rosenbluth claim that there was no theoretical presumption that the Giffen case was in any sense 'unlikely', however infrequently the case actually seemed to arise. He offered an alternative explanation:

> The paradoxical aspect of the Giffen paradox is the inability of demand theory to explain why Giffen goods are apparently so rare. The resolution of the paradox arises from the distinction between the shape of the market demand curves and the sequence of equilibrium prices that will be observed in markets in which quantity supplied changes. The sense in which the Giffen case is 'unlikely' to occur is that the probability of identifying a Giffen good is less than the probability that such a good exists. (p. 809)

Dougan maintained that Marshall's law of demand was indeed true, as a law governing markets, but that the Giffen case may well be more commonplace than had been supposed. In effect, he offered yet another interpretation of a paradox which was continuing to pose substantial problems for demand theorists and around which no consensus was forming. The lack of progress was highlighted in 1984, when Silberberg and Walker offered a modern analysis of Giffen's paradox. In this they argued, first, that (contrary to Mayston 1976) Marshall had indeed assumed additive utilities in his theoretical treatment of demand; second, that (contrary to Stigler 1950) the paradox was consistent with this assumption; third, that (contrary to Gramm 1970) the paradox was not an allusion to an exceptional empirical possibility; fourth, that (under Marshall's assumptions) there can only be one non-inferior good ('meat and the more expensive farinaceous foods' (?)); and fifth, that it can be demonstrated mathematically that the marginal utility of income actually falls when the price of a Giffen good rises.

* * *

In reviewing the literature on the Giffen paradox it is somewhat paradoxical to discover that far more interest has been shown in the phenomenon in the years since 1945 than in the thirty years immediately following Giffen's death in 1910. Certainly, any possibility of witnessing the paradox in Britain or in the United States was greater in the interwar years and had effectively disappeared by 1940. Interest in the subject, therefore, has been inversely related to the probability that such behaviour can occur among the poorer sections of society in both countries.

There are factors which help to explain this apparent paradox. The Stigler–Prest debate of 1947–8; the 1950s interest in Marshall's demand curve and in utility theory generally; the new consumer theories of the 1960s: all served to draw attention to the paradox, either directly or indirectly. This in contrast to the 1920s and 1930s, when academic preoccupations were very different and when Giffen and his paradox had, for the most part, been forgotten. The greater interest shown in the years since 1945 has added to a meagre literature but has left many questions unanswered. Stigler's 1947 research was, by his own admission, far from comprehensive and should ideally have served as a springboard for a more detailed investigation into the origins of the paradox. In the event, no such studies materialised, and further research into the paradox statement and into the nineteenth-century conditions which might have produced such behaviour has been remarkable only by its absence.

Whilst interest in historical research has been negligible, the paradox has nevertheless continued to interest economists, who need to reconcile it with the laws of classical demand theory, and mathematical economists, who see it as an abstract curiosity which is from time to time acknowledged. This emphasis on theory is not surprising as the vastly improved living conditions in Britain and the United States have offered no real opportunity for domestic empirical research. However, the theoretical discussion itself has been unproductive in that we are today little nearer to accommodating the paradox within demand theory than we were in 1895.

The re-emergence of the paradox as a topic of some limited interest after 1945 did serve to highlight its reputation as the major exception to the law of demand. This recognition has in turn merited a small place for the phenomenon in many of the economic textbooks which have appeared in more recent years. These short references and footnotes, however, are often inaccurate and misleading. As we have already seen, Dwyer and Lindsay (1984) challenged the 'fallacious consensus' which seemed to be emerging that the paradox had been observed during the 1845–9 Irish potato famine and that it was the Irish potato rather than English bread which had produced such behaviour. The case for the 'potato paradox' was clearly not sustainable, as Dwyer and Lindsay demonstrated. Kohli (1986) supported their conclusions (if not their precise reasoning), and the argument linking the paradox to the Irish famines is now effectively discredited. A problem however remains — nineteenth-century Ireland is still commonly quoted in economic textbooks as the source of Giffen's observation and this can only serve to misdirect and confuse any future research.

References to Giffen himself in more recent literature are often equally ill-informed. He has been variously described as an eighteenth-century economist who 'came across an example in Ireland' and as a British army officer stationed in Ireland in the nineteenth century (it is, perhaps, worth noting that at the start of the 1845–9 Irish famine Giffen was eight years old). He is also frequently referred to as English rather than Scottish, an error to which Giffen himself would have taken the greatest exception.

Twentieth-century concern both with Robert Giffen and with his paradox has been, at best, spasmodic. As a result, and as the last two chapters have shown, little real progress has been made towards a better understanding either of the man or of the exceptional consumer behaviour with which his name is most closely associated. It is possible to argue, of course, that in any event we know enough about an unremarkable and largely insignificant statistician and should concern ourselves no longer with a paradox which is now consigned to the history books. The next and last chapter, however, argues for some further reconsideration.

References

Alford, R.F.G. (1956) 'Marshall's demand curve', *Economica*, Vol. 23 (February), pp. 23–48.
Boland, L.A. (1977) 'Giffen goods, market prices and testability', *Australian Economic Papers*, Vol. 16 (June), pp. 72–85.
Bopp, A.E. (1983) 'The demand for kerosene: a modern Giffen good', *Applied Economics*, Vol. 15, pp. 459–67.
Bowley, A.L. (1940) 'Working-class expenditure', *Economic Journal*, Vol. 50 (December), pp. 517–24.
Burnett, J. (1979) *Plenty and Want*, Scolar Press (first published by Nelson 1966).

De Alessi, L. (1968) 'A methodological appraisal of Giffen's paradox', *Weltwirtschaftliches Archiv*, Vol. 101.

Dougan, W.R. (1982) 'Giffen goods and the law of demand', *Journal of Political Economy*, Vol. 90, No. 4 (August), pp. 809–15.

Dwyer, G.P. Jr. and Lindsay, C.M. (1984) 'Robert Giffen and the Irish potato', *American Economic Review*, Vol. 74, No. 1 (March), pp. 188–92.

Friedman, M. (1949) 'The Marshallian demand curve', *Journal of Political Economy*, Vol. 57, No. 6 (December), pp. 463–95.

Gramm, W.P. (1970) 'Giffen's paradox and the Marshallian demand curve', *Manchester School of Economic and Social Studies*, Vol. 38 (March), pp. 65–71.

Hicks, J.R. (1956) *A Revision of Demand Theory*, Clarendon Press.

Johnson, W.E. (1913) 'The pure theory of utility curves', *Economic Journal*, Vol. 23, pp. 483–513.

Kohli, U. (1986) 'Robert Giffen and the Irish potato: note', *American Economic Review*, Vol. 76, No. 3 (June), pp. 539–42.

Lancaster, K.J. (1966) 'A new approach to consumer theory', *Journal of Political Economy*, Vol. 74, pp. 132–57.

Lipsey, R.G. and Rosenbluth, G. (1971) 'A contribution to the new theory of demand: a rehabilitation of the Giffen good', *Canadian Journal of Economics*, Vol. 4, No. 2 (May), pp. 131–63.

Mayston, D.J. (1976) 'On the nature of marginal utility — a neo-Marshallian theory of demand', *Economic Journal*, Vol. 86 (September), pp. 493–507.

Pareto, V. (1897) *Le Cours d'Economie Politique*, Vol. 2, Librairie de l'Université, Lausanne.

Prest, A.R. (1948) 'Notes on the history of the Giffen paradox: comment', *Journal of Political Economy*, Vol. 56 (February), pp. 58–60.

Samuelson, P. (1946) 'Comparative statics and the logic of economic maximising', *Review of Economic Studies*, Vol. 14, pp. 41–3.

Silberberg, E. and Walker, D.A. (1984) 'A modern analysis of Giffen's paradox', *International Economic Review*, Vol. 25, No. 3 (October), pp. 687–94.

Steindl, F.G. (1973) 'Money and bonds as Giffen goods', *Manchester School of Economic and Social Studies*, Vol. 41, pp. 418–24.

Stigler, G. (1945) 'The cost of subsistence', *Journal of Farm Economics*, Vol. 27 (May), pp. 303–14.

Stigler, G. (1947) 'Notes on the history of the Giffen paradox', *Journal of Political Economy*, Vol. 55 (April), pp. 152–6.

Stigler, G. (1948) 'A reply', *Journal of Political Economy*, Vol. 56 (February), pp. 61–2.

Stigler, G. (1950) 'The development of utility theory II', *Journal of Political Economy*, Vol. 58, No. 5, pp. 373–96.

Vandermeulen, D.C. (1972) 'Upward sloping demand curves without the Giffen paradox', *American Economic Review*, Vol. 62 (June), pp. 453–8.

CHAPTER 9

Epilogue

This book has looked in some detail at the life and work of Robert Giffen and at the paradox which is claimed by many to be the single genuine exception to the law of demand. It is now possible to reassess the man, the Giffen paradox and the place of this paradox in the economics of the late twentieth century.

In so far as Robert Giffen himself is concerned, his books, articles and speeches show that as a statistician and economist he has at least been underestimated. Certainly Stigler's view that Giffen was not a subtle analyst cannot be supported in any way by what we know of his work in the later part of the nineteenth century. But he was not alone in arguing that Giffen's contribution to economics was trivial. Robertson (1952) wrote of the 'despised Giffen', referring in particular to the critical comments of Rostow (1948) who had little time either for Giffen's analytical skills or for his competence as an economist. Robertson himself was more generous in his treatment of Giffen and indeed had good reason to be more cautious.

First, Giffen's skills as a statistician are not in doubt. Sir Alfred Bateman, Giffen's successor at the Board of Trade, described him in 1910 as 'the most popular, if not the ablest, statistician of modern times' and, in his obituary to Giffen in the same year, Edgeworth quoted and endorsed the opinion of 'one who is among the highest authorities on the application of the mathematical theory of error to practical statistics' that:

> With an acute perception of the things that were measured or unmeasurable, he [Giffen] first surrounded the official statistics with an atmosphere of caution, and then cleared away the mist by the use of bold estimates. For these estimates he had an arithmetical sense almost amounting to genius, a feeling for the probable error of the factors used, and a courageous rejection of measurements where the

inaccuracy was too great. He had an intuitive feeling for the relative importance of numbers. He used to express his conclusion as to the adequacy of the data by saying he could, or could not, 'give a figure'. He appears to have had little or no knowledge of the modern mathematical theory of statistics, but his arithmetical strength was so strong that he was able to proceed safely and with knowledge through calculations whose validity could only be established mathematically. (pp. 320–1)

Giffen's reputation as a statistician was first established through the work he carried out for Goschen on the Local Taxation Report to the Treasury, published in March 1871 –– a report which was followed by his appointment as Chief of the Statistical Department and Controller of Corn Returns at the Board of Trade, in 1876. At the same time, his connection with the Royal Statistical Society enhanced his reputation with a wider audience, not least for his ability to develop new approaches to statistical methodology. As an example, his book *The Growth of Capital* (1889) first established the convention of estimating a nation's total capital stock from income tax returns — a system which, in modified form, is still used to this day. His success as a statistician over some forty years was such that Edgeworth, no casual bestower of praise, claimed that Giffen 'deserves to be honoured with the masters of Statistical Science' (p. 321).

Giffen's contribution to economics and to political economy was equally impressive. When his book *Stock Exchange Securities* was published in 1877, for example, its impact was substantial, not least upon Alfred Marshall. Eshag (1963) has pointed out that in this book:

> . . . ten years before Marshall gave his evidence before the Gold and Silver Commission, Giffen explains very clearly the relationship which subsists between the bankers' cash reserves and deposits. Thus, he writes 'The amount which banks or other intermediaries can lend is limited by the amount of real money at command. Say a banker has to keep half the amount of his liabilities in cash, the limit to the credit he can give is measured by this necessity. The moment his deposits are twice the amount of his cash, the amount of his lending must cease'. It is interesting to note that in commenting on this passage, Marshall scribbled the following note on his personal copy of Giffen's book. 'This is important, and perhaps not so well brought out elsewhere'. (p. 16)

Later, in his evidence to the Gold and Silver Commission, Marshall acknowledged that Giffen was also the first to have dealt with the relationship between bankers' money and the amount of currency in circulation and that other economists had not really examined this relationship in any detail: 'The most pregnant hints on it are, I think, those given by Mr Giffen in his *Stock Exchange Securities*. I do not think that his solution is complete, but he seems to have pointed towards the right solution' (Minutes, 9638).

Marshall was, in fact, less than honest in this evidence to the Commission, for Giffen had developed his argument in two later articles, written in 1879 and 1885. These articles (published in 1886) provided a comprehensive explanation of the role of the rate of discount in settling the equilibrium between gold supply and the price level, and they bore a striking resemblance to the solution proposed by Marshall in 1887 and 1888. Eshag concludes:

> It can thus be seen that every aspect of the problem of the *modus operandi* of the quantity theory under a banking system and the role played by the rate of discount in that process had been discussed by Giffen in his publications of 1877 and 1886. In view of this fact, and Marshall's evident familiarity with the work of Giffen, there can be very little doubt about the historical significance of the latter's writings and the influence exercised by him on Marshall. (p. 18)

Giffen's contributions to economics were recognised elsewhere. His papers advising on the relative merits of investment, both in Britain and overseas, were much appreciated and acted upon by an investing public who had the greatest respect for his abilities as a market analyst. In 1883 Joseph Chamberlain, then President of the Board of Trade, acknowledged that Giffen was, in fact, the author of the new bankruptcy law which had passed through Parliament. And in 1886, under the pseudonym 'Economist', he contributed several articles to *The Statist* in which he proposed a scheme for buying out Irish landlords and which was, in large measure, passed into law in 1903.

Giffen also joined in the late-nineteenth-century debate on the relative merits of bimetallism, arguing in 1892 that such a policy was absurd as well as impracticable. On this subject, as already mentioned, *The Economist* later pointed out that a single letter written by Giffen to *The Times* had proved so powerful and damaging to the bimetallist cause that it effectively ended any prospect of its adoption by Britain (16 April, 1910, p. 835).

It is easy to find many other examples of Giffen's influence on economic affairs and on the development of economic thought in the last century. Given this substantial evidence, why then has he been largely neglected as a serious contributor? Perhaps the most significant reason for this neglect lies in the fact that he was in no sense an academic nor had he ever been academically trained in economics. Compared with men of the stature of Marshall and Edgeworth, therefore, he could easily be seen as an amateur — a statistician of undoubted arithmetical skills who had presumed to dabble in economic matters but who, lacking any mathematical or classical education, was unable, almost by definition, to make anything other than uninformed or trivial contributions to the developing science.

Certainly, Giffen's reputation as an economist has worsened over the years, a fact which would have surprised many of his friends. His contemporaries had, in fact, been more generous, acknowledging that he was unconventional but giving full credit to his work. Thorold Rogers (1888) wrote of him: 'The student who is anxious to go beyond the common chatter of text-books and manuals, will learn more and better political economy from Mr Giffen's essays than he would if he browsed for ever on the thorns and thistles of abstract political economy' (p. 8), and Giffen's common sense approach to economic reasoning was admired by many other eminent economists of his day. In the final tribute to Giffen, *The Statist* put the matter most succinctly:

> Again, doubt has been expressed whether Sir Robert ever was a strict economist. To the real economist the doubt is amusing . . . Sir Robert was an economist in the true sense. He has not swallowed what he found in books. He was, of course, a careful student of the great economic thinkers. But at the same time he thought out for himself the theories he accepted. He recognised where economists had carried their theories too far, and he also perceived where popular economists had failed to carry their theories far enough. (16 April, 1910, p. 803)

Given these endorsements, the case for some reconsideration of Giffen's contribution to nineteenth-century economics and to the development of the subject would not be difficult to make.

* * *

Robert Giffen undoubtedly concerned himself with the economic matters of his day, but what of the paradox with which he is particularly associated?

The appearance of the paradox in the 1895 edition of *Principles* is explained by Marshall's debate with Nicholson, Edgeworth and others over the significance of the marginal utility of money. The exchange of views in 1893–4 convinced Marshall that an additional section should be added to the chapter on value and utility, pointing out that while it was seldom necessary to take account of changes in the purchaser's command of money, Robert Giffen had in fact discovered a rare exception.

Second, it has been argued here that we should look to London and to the 1860s, in particular, in the search for evidence of nineteenth-century paradox behaviour. The middle years of that decade saw the poor having to face three years of steadily rising bread prices and brought destitution to the capital on a large scale. Certainly, we have enough circumstantial evidence to suggest that paradox behaviour was occurring on a significant scale in the East End of London in 1867 and 1868.

It is certain also that conditions similar to those found in London existed in many other industrial cities throughout Britain and that the very poor would have reacted in much the same way when faced with frequent increases in the price of bread. London had no 'exclusive rights' to the paradox: it must be seen as a phenomenon which could and did occur in many towns and cities across the country. However, Giffen's evidence of such behaviour surely came from London and from the conditions which he and others saw around them in the capital.

In so far as the paradox itself is concerned, what is its relevance today? There is no doubt that the nineteenth-century phenomenon has disappeared in Britain and in other affluent industrialised countries. With the protection offered by the welfare state and with the vastly improved standards of living 'enjoyed' by the poor (who are now rich by nineteenth-century standards), the desperation which drove people to eat nothing but bread has thankfully gone. This has undoubtedly contributed to the lack of interest in what many now see as a historical curiosity. Yet in another respect the paradox remains relevant, even within today's affluent societies.

Whilst the paradox observed by Giffen has disappeared, the behaviour it describes is still with us, albeit in greatly changed circumstances. We now recognise that it does not require either a staple foodstuff or abject poverty for it to exist and that a 'Giffen effect' can and does occur over a whole range of buying decisions — taken within a given (if generous) budget when one product is held to be inferior to another in any particular yet important respect. These purchase decisions are common enough to call into question the very idea that such behaviour is paradoxical: indeed, Marshall's question to Edgeworth, in citing the example of transportation, remains valid, 'Where is the paradox?'

The paradox, therefore, remains relevant within affluent societies but has taken a modified form. Today, it describes behaviour associated not with absolute poverty and the need to survive but with budgeted expenditures within adequate incomes, and with wants rather than needs. In this sense, Giffen goods and Giffenesque behaviour will continue to be significant in the most prosperous societies.

Looking beyond the affluence of industrialised countries to the underdeveloped and developing economies of the world, the relevance of the paradox becomes very different. There, poverty and hunger can exist on a scale equal to and beyond that suffered by the poor of nineteenth-century Britain, and the Giffen paradox retains all its original meaning in describing the behaviour of near-destitute people faced with increases in the price of their essential foods. Conditions necessary to paradox behaviour exist in abundance. State provision of welfare can be insignificant or even non-existent, and people survive only on what little income they or their families can secure. A high proportion of family income has to be spent on food but is often unable to bring a sufficient variety into the diet — indeed, it is not unusual to find individuals and families subsisting entirely on a single food, with meat or vegetables added as a very occasional luxury. The basic food on which people depend can vary greatly. Bread, potatoes and rice, among others, serve as staples in different parts of the world. As in Victorian Britain, however, overdependence on one item in the diet brings ill-health and malnutrition. Diseases such as pellagra and kwashiorkor, for example, attack people whose diets consist almost entirely of staple foods such as maize or cassava and who are too poor to enrich the diet with meat, fish or whole-grain cereals.

Descriptions of the way of life of the urban poor in developing countries often show a remarkable similarity to the conditions endured by British workers one hundred years ago. In her study of life among the poor in Cairo, Wikan (1976) describes the attempts made by families to subsist on far-from-adequate incomes:

> With these price levels the families have to make do with a diet consisting almost exclusively of rice, bread and vegetables, with tea as the daily, almost the only, drink. One must bear in mind the fact that the men with their demanding jobs need a reasonable number of calories per day and also that women, in order to realize the cultural ideal of obesity, eat disproportionately large amounts. On the few occasions when these people taste meat — it can be from once a week to once a month — the meal consists mainly of rice, tomatoes and bread with only two to three tiny, precious pieces of meat per person. They are obsessed with their diet themselves, and fantasies and dreams about food are ever-recurring topics of conversation. They express a clear understanding of the need for nutritious food (*cesa*) which they define as meat, fish, eggs, milk and cheese. They blame malnutrition as the main reason for their physical and mental fatigue. (pp. 33–4)

Wikan also found that when money was needed for essential non-food items, a standard solution was to reduce the outlay on food even further by eating only rice or beans with bread. Living conditions such as these are clearly little removed from those of Giffen's original paradox: the location is changed, a cultural difference introduced (the desire to be obese), but the essential ingredients exist for such exceptional consumer behaviour to occur.

Any progress away from poverty that developing countries make can also be quickly reversed. As an example, between 1982 and 1987, the number of Mexicans with no jobs or regular income doubled. Average family incomes were, by 1987, not enough to buy even half the basic food 'basket' established by the local social services institutes, and the consumption of proteins went down by some 40 per cent. Under such conditions, individuals and families are quickly forced back to dependence on a staple diet and eat little if any high protein foods. And if the deterioration continues, then paradox conditions reappear.

Empirical research into the validity and incidence of the Giffen paradox could still be sensibly carried out in those parts of the world where hunger and poverty are the norm rather than the exception. Indeed, some economists have already accepted that the paradox exists in developing countries. Hardwick, Khan and Langmead (1982) quote rice consumption in Bangladesh as 'Giffen' and others have pointed to the Indian sub-continent as capable of demonstrating the existence of the paradox. Similarly, Dwyer and Lindsay (1984) concluded that 'the place to look for a Giffen good is not a peasant economy engaged in subsistence farming, but in poor communities that import most of their food. Has anyone considered rice in Singapore?' (p. 191).

The paradox may well survive in those free market economies which, though prosperous, allow for great differences in the distribution of income between rich and poor, and where extremes of wealth and poverty can therefore be found side by side. At first sight, official statistics in such societies can be misleading. *The 1984–85 Report of the Household Expenditure Survey*, published by the Hong Kong Government's Department of Census and Statistics, showed that within the budget for food prepared at home by the poorest sample group, only 11.8 per cent was spent on rice — a statistic which rose to 29 per cent for rice and fresh vegetables taken together. Overall, some 59 per cent of all spending by this group went on foodstuffs.

On this evidence, there is no reason to suppose that paradox conditions exist in Hong Kong, but there are grounds for caution. The Survey's poorest sample group were those households with monthly expenditures in the range HK$2,000–6,999, and the most affluent were those spending HK$10,000–24,999. It was noted that 'the remaining households (outside the above expenditure ranges) were excluded from the coverage of the indexes *because of their distinctly different expenditure patterns'*. The exclusion of the very rich and very poor was, in fact, highly significant because it recognised and omitted not only potential conspicuous consumers at the top of the range but also those in real poverty, whose monthly expenditure fell far short of HK$2,000 per month and who were seen to be significantly 'different' in their expected purchasing behaviour. For the very poor who were not included in the Survey, rice purchases would have represented the larger part of their total expenditure on food, leaving them with little extra for 'luxuries', and it is within such groups that any search for a modern Giffen paradox needs to be directed.

The search need not be confined to Bangladesh, Singapore or Hong Kong. Conditions in many parts of Africa and Latin America are often comparable with those of the Far East in terms of poverty and deprivation, and there is no reason to suppose that the paradox could not just as easily be seen in Lagos and Lima as in Dhaka. Indeed, wherever poverty drives people to survive for the most part on one staple food and offers them little prospect of a more varied diet, then increases in the price of the staple will produce conditions under which Robert Giffen's paradox could occur.

References

Bateman, A.E. (1910) 'Obituary', *Journal of the Royal Statistical Society*, Vol. 73 (May), pp. 529–33.

Dwyer, G.P. Jr. and Lindsay, C.M. (1984) 'Robert Giffen and the Irish potato', *American Economic Review*, Vol. 74, No. 1 (March), pp. 188–92.

Edgeworth, F.Y. (1910) 'Obituary: Sir Robert Giffen', *Economic Journal*, Vol. 20 (June), pp. 318–21. The obituary is unsigned but attributed to Edgeworth.

Eshag, E. (1963) *From Marshall to Keynes: An Essay on the Monetary Theory of the Cambridge School*, Blackwell.

Giffen, R. (1877) *Stock Exchange Securities*, George Bell & Sons.

Giffen R. (1879) 'The effects on trade of the supply of coinage', in *Essays in Finance*, 2nd Series (1886), George Bell & Sons, pp. 89–104.

Giffen, R. (1885) 'Gold supply: the rate of discount, and prices', in *Essays in Finance*, 2nd Series (1886), George Bell & Sons, pp. 37–88.

Giffen, R. (1889) *The Growth of Capital*, George Bell & Sons.

Giffen, R. (1892) *The Case Against Bimetallism*, George Bell & Sons.

Hardwick, P., Khan, B. and Langmead, J. (1982) *An Introduction to Modern Economics*, Longman.

Robertson, D.H. (1952) *Utility and All That and Other Essays*, George Allen & Unwin.

Rogers, J.E.T. (1888) *The Economic Interpretation of History*, T. Fisher Unwin.

Rostow, W.W. (1948) *British Economy of the Nineteenth Century*, Clarendon Press.
Wikan, U. (1976) *Fattigfolk i Cairo*, Glydendal, Norsk Forlag. English
translation by A. Henning (1980) *Life Among the Poor in Cairo*,
Tavistock Publications.

Bibliographical Notes

It is not possible to draw together a complete bibliography of Robert Giffen's work. He was, throughout his life, a prolific author, writing books and articles, presenting papers to learned societies, compiling reports for Select Committees and Royal Commissions and losing no opportunity to write letters to the press on matters of current controversy. However, a major problem is that many of his articles, tracts and reports were, on his own admission, published anonymously, particularly after his appointment to a politically sensitive post at the Board of Trade, in 1876.

Given these limitations, the following list nevertheless covers the greater part of Giffen's published work and shows the extent to which he contributed to political, economic and social debate. His interests were demonstrably catholic and he involved himself in many of the important issues of his time. These bibliographical notes serve to illustrate his many interests and concerns.

Books

American Railways as Investments (1872) Cracroft's Investment Tracts, Stanford.

Stock Exchange Securities (1877) George Bell & Sons. The second edition (1879) was enlarged by an Appendix of Evidence given before the Royal Commission of the Stock Exchange.

Essays in Finance, 1st Series (1880) George Bell & Sons.

Essays in Finance, 2nd Series (1886) George Bell & Sons.

The Growth of Capital (1889) George Bell & Sons.

The Case Against Bimetallism (1892) George Bell & Sons.

Economic Inquiries and Studies (1904) George Bell & Sons.
Statistics (1913) Macmillan & Co. Published posthumously and edited by Henry Higgs and George Udny Yule. Giffen wrote the first draft of the book between 1898 and 1900.

Articles

Many of Giffen's journal articles appear also in the first or second series of his *Essays in Finance*, published in 1880 and 1886, and/or in the two volumes of *Economic Inquiries and Studies* (1904). Where this is the case, and to avoid repetition, reference is made either to 'EF1' or 'EF2' and/or to 'EIS' after the name of the journal in which the article originally appeared, and its date of publication. Certain papers were written specifically for these books and these are also indicated using the same abbreviations.

'The reduction of the National Debt' (1867) EF1.
'Financial questions for the reformed Parliament', *Fortnightly Review* (1867).
'Russian railways', *Fortnightly Review* (1868).
'The question of Central Asia', *Fortnightly Review* (1868).
'Mr Gladstone's work in finance', *Fortnightly Review* (1869) EF1, EIS.
'Revivers of British industry' (1869). Written anonymously. Acknowledged by Giffen in the Preface to EIS.
'Taxes on land', *Fortnightly Review* (1871) EF1, EIS.
'The cost of the Franco-German war' (1872) EF1, EIS. Privately published.
'The depreciation of gold since 1848' (1872) EF1, EIS. Written as a sequel to a series of articles on the production and movement of gold published in *The Economist*.
'Why the depression of trade is so much greater in raw material producing countries than in the manufacturing countries' (1875) EF1.
'The taxation and representation of Ireland', *The Economist* (1876) EF1, EIS.
'The depreciation of silver', *Journal of the Statistical Society* (1876) EF1, as 'Notes on the depreciation of silver'. The paper was originally read by Giffen at the Social Science Congress, Liverpool, October 1876 as 'The causes and effects of the depreciation of silver, how far is it an evil, and what are the means of remedying the evil?'
'The liquidations of 1873–76', *Fortnightly Review* (1877) EF1, EIS.
'Foreign competition' (1877) EF1, EIS.
'The excess of imports' (1877) EF1.

'Recent accumulations of capital in the United Kingdom', *Journal of the Statistical Society* (1878) EF1.

'The case against bimetallism', *Fortnightly Review* (1879) EF1.

'On the fall of prices of commodities in recent years', *Journal of the Statistical Society* (1879). This paper was later published in EF1 and in EIS as 'On the fall of prices of commodities in 1873–79'.

'The effects on trade of the supply of coinage' (1879) EF2.

'The new protection cry' (1879). Written as a political tract under the pseudonym 'Economist' and attributed to Giffen.

'Bagehot as an economist', *Fortnightly Review* (1880).

'Bank reserves' (1881) EF2.

'The foreign trade of the United States' (1881) EF2.

'The use of import and export statistics', *Journal of the Statistical Society* (1882) EF2, EIS.

'The utility of common statistics', *Journal of the Statistical Society* (1882) EF2, EIS.

'The progress of the working classes in the last half century', *Journal of the Statistical Society* (1883) EF2, EIS. Giffen read the paper as his Inaugural Address as President of the Statistical Society (Session 1883–4) in November 1883.

'Foreign manufactures and English trade' (1885) EF2. Originally published in the form of letters to *The Times* in answer to Lord Dunraven's comments in the course of a fair-trade debate, House of Lords, November 1884.

'Trade depression and low prices', *Contemporary Review* (1885) EF2.

'Some general uses of statistical knowledge', *Journal of the Statistical Society* (1885) EF2. Read at the Jubilee Meeting of the Statistical Society, 23 June 1885.

'Gold supply; the rate of discount, and prices' (1885) EF2.

'Further notes on the progress of the working classes', *Journal of the Statistical Society* (1886) EF2. The paper was read before the Statistical Society in January 1886.

'The economic value of Ireland to Great Britain', *Nineteenth Century* (1886) EIS.

'The growth and distribution of wealth' (1887). Contribution to a book compiled by T.H. Ward (ed.) *The Reign of Queen Victoria*.

'The recent rate of material progress in England', *Journal of the Statistical Society* (1887) EIS. Given as an address as President of Section F at the British Association meeting, Manchester, 1887.

'Recent changes in prices and incomes compared', *Journal of the Royal Statistical Society* (1888) EIS.

'A problem in money', *Nineteenth Century* (1889).

'The gross and net gain of rising wages', *Contemporary Review* (1889) EIS.

'The American silver bubble', *Nineteenth Century* (1890).

'On the accumulation of capital in the United Kingdom', *Journal of the Royal Statistical Society* (1890).

'The Gresham Law', *Economic Journal* (1891). This article also appears as 'A note on the Gresham Law' in EIS.

'Fancy monetary standards', *Economic Journal* (1892) EIS.

'On international statistical comparisons', *Economic Journal* (1892) EIS. Read at a meeting of the Australasian Association for the Advancement of Science, Hobart, January 1892.

'Depression corrected', *Edinburgh Review* (1895).

'Protectionist victories and free trade successes' (1897) EIS. Originally a speech to the North Staffordshire Chamber of Commerce at Stoke, 15 December 1897.

'Monetary chaos', *Nineteenth Century* (1897).

'Protection for manufactures in new countries', *Economic Journal* (1898) EIS.

'Indian gold standard problem', *Economic Journal* (1898).

'The relative growth of the component parts of the Empire', *Royal Colonial Institute Journal* (1899) EIS.

'The excess of imports', *Journal of the Royal Statistical Society* (1899). Read before the Society, 17 January 1899.

'Consols in a great war', *Economic Journal* (1899) EIS.

'The coming wheat scarcity', *Nature* (1899). Review of an essay on 'The wheat problem' by Sir William Crookes, delivered as Presidential Address to the British Association, Bristol, 1898.

'Our trade prosperity and the outlook', *Economic Journal* (1900).

'Some economic aspects of the South African war', *Economic Journal* (1900) EIS.

'The statistical century' (1900) EIS. Address at the Annual Dinner of the Manchester Statistical Society, 17 October 1900.

'The importance of general statistical ideas' (1901) EIS. Address to the British Association in Glasgow.

'Further notes on the aspects of war', *Economic Journal* (1901).

'Are we living on capital?' (1901) EIS. Read before the Institute of Bankers, 22 May 1901.

'The standard of strength for our army: a business estimate', *Nineteenth Century and After* (1901) EIS.

'A financial retrospect — 1861–1901', *Journal of the Royal Statistical Society* (1902) EIS. Read before the Royal Statistical Society, 18 March 1902, drawing together letters to *The Times* on the 'Financial outlook' (7, 9 and 10 January), then developing a 40-year retrospect.

'The dream of a British Zollverein', *Nineteenth Century and After* (1902) EIS.

'The wealth of the Empire and how it should be used', *Journal of the Royal Statistical Society* (1903) EIS. Read before the Economics and Statistics Section of the British Association, Southport, September 1903.

'Imperial policy and free trade', *Nineteenth Century and After* (1903).

'Ineffectual preferences', *Nineteenth Century and After* (1904).

'The present economic conditions and outlook for the United Kingdom' (1904) EIS.

'Local extravagance and imperial burdens', *Contemporary Review* (1905).

'The prospects of Liberal finance', *Nineteenth Century and After* (1906).

'Is the British Empire safe?: a note on national service', *Nineteenth Century and After* (1906).

'English commerce in a naval war', *Nineteenth Century and After* (1907).

Evidence to Select Committees and Royal Commissions

Giffen gave evidence to many Committees and Commissions during his time at the Board of Trade and was invited, on occasion, to sit as a member and to question witnesses. His testimony is included in reports of the following inquiries:

Select Committee on the Depreciation of Silver, 1876.
The Stock Exchange Commission, 1878.
Official Statistics Committee, 1878–9.
Select Committee on Sugar Industries 1878–80.
Royal Commission on Agriculture, 1881–2.
Select Committee on the Channel Tunnel, 1882–3.
Royal Commission on the Depression of Trade and Industry, 1885–6.
Royal Commission on Gold and Silver, 1886–8.
Select Committee on Corn Averages, 1888.
Royal Commission on Labour, 1892–4.
Royal Commission on Agricultural Depression, 1893–7.
Local Taxation Commission, 1898.

Giffen's letters to *The Times*

After his appointment as a senior official at the Board of Trade, Giffen used *The Times* more than any other newspaper to join in the debates over matters of current interest and controversy. The following is a record of his more important leading articles and correspondence with the newspaper. Many of the letters matched the publication dates of Giffen articles and reports on the same topics, and allowed him an opportunity both to reply to his critics (some of whose letters to the newspaper are also included below) and to further develop his arguments.

'The fall in prices of commodities', 22 January 1879.
'Sugar industries', 12 July 1880.
'On the sugar bounties', 24 May 1881.
'Bad harvests and agricultural depression', 7 January 1882.
'Population statistics and political thought', 22 November 1882.
'Australian statistics', 29 December 1882.
'Progress of the working classes', 26 November 1883.
'On the sugar bounties', 18 and 23 June 1884.
'Is the increase of foreign manufactures injurious to English trade?', 27 November, 12, 26 and 31 December 1884.
'On fair trade', 5, 7 and 9 January 1885.
'The alleged over-taxation of Ireland', 12 and 29 April 1886.
'The progress of the working classes', 30 April 1886.
'The currency question', 18 August 1886.
'On the address at the British Association', 9 September 1887.
'Paper on recent changes in prices and incomes compared', 19 December 1888.
'Report on sugar bounties', 26 June and 8 July 1889.
'The accumulation of capital', 18 December 1889.
'On the inevitable results of universal bimetallism', 26 December 1889.
'On accumulations of capital', 2 January 1890.
'On bimetallism', 2 and 31 January 1890.
'On unsaleable silver', 4 and 6 January 1890.
'The alleged bimetallism of France, 1803–1873', 11 February 1890.
'On emigration', 23 April 1890.
'On emigration', 7 October 1892.
'Fishery statistics', 11 September 1893.
'Royal Statistical Society', 21 November 1894.
'On the Royal Commission on Agriculture', 7 August 1897.
'On bimetallism and the Indian mints', 25 September 1897.
'On the bank and silver', 5 October 1897.
'On the government and bimetallism', 15 October 1897.
'Appreciation of gold', 16 and 26 October 1897.
'On free trade', 17 December 1897.
'Our commercial interests in the Far East', 24 and 26 March, 2 and 12 April 1898.
'On Indian currency', 12, 19 and 27 May and 6 June 1898.
'On the uses of statistics', 29 November 1898.
'On the excess of imports', 18 and 21 January 1899.
'On the relative growth of the component parts of the Empire', 15 February 1899.

'On pauperism', 8 December 1899.
'On European expansion', 18 October 1900.
'On army reform', 26 February and 14 March 1901.
'On the Liberal Party', 5 July 1901.
'On the financial outlook', 7, 9 and 10 January, 19 and 31 March 1902.
'On customs duties and free trade', 2 April 1902.
'On preferential arrangements', 17 June 1902.
'On the Venezuelan mess', 18 December 1902, 27 January, 23 February 1903.
'Industrial trusts', 15 January 1903.
'On preferential tariffs', 28 May 1903.
'How far are our self-governing colonies really protectionist?', 14 July 1903.
'Indian poverty', 21 September 1903.
'Mr Chamberlain's statistics', 24, 27 and 29 October and 9 November 1903.
'On universal training', 23 March 1906.
'On the Royal Commission on Local Taxation', 23 July 1909.
'On some budget notes', 12 August 1909.
'On free trade unionists and tariff reform candidates', 17 January 1910.

'The Giffen Collection'

A collection of letters written to Giffen, together with manuscripts, articles and other papers, is held at the British Library of Political and Economic Science, London School of Economics. The manuscripts give some indication of the width of Giffen's interests, including work on 'A legend of Strathaven Castle' and other articles on Strathaven, a 'true' ghost story, poems, and papers on Cicero, on househunting and housebuilding, on the career and character of Cobden and on the Political Economy Club.

The collection comprises five volumes:

Volume 1: Letters to Sir Robert Giffen, 1861–1900.
Volume 2: Letters to Sir Robert Giffen, 1901–1910.
Volume 3: Articles by Sir Robert Giffen.
Volume 4: Miscellaneous letters and papers.
Volume 5: Newscuttings, etc.

Index

Royal Economic Society, 19, 58
Royal Statistical Society
  see Statistical Society
Russell, C.E.B., 102

Salaman, R.N., 65, 68
Salford, 101, 102
Salisbury, Lord, 91
Samuelson, Paul, 67–8, 117, 121
Sartor Resartus, 37
Saturday Review, 15
Savings, 32
Scavengers in London, 83
Schultz, H., 111, 112
Scotland
  diet in, 69–71
  Highlands and Islands of, 69
  Lowlands of, 70
Shaw-Lefevre, John, 10
Shetlands, 70
Shove, G.F., 113
Sidmouth, Lord, 95, 98
Silberberg, E., 126
Singapore, 137, 138
Smith, Adam, 34, 51
Socialists, 45, 48
Spectator, 15, 42, 46, 47
Statist, 16, 18, 24n, 132, 133
Statistical Society, 16, 17, 19, 20,
  23, 26, 35, 38, 39, 42, 58, 61,
  62, 77, 87, 90, 91, 131
  *Journal of the (Royal) Statistical
  Society*, 19, 23n, 61, 62
Steindl, F.G., 124
Stigler, G., 8, 9, 10, 11, 12, 57, 117,
  118, 119, 120, 126, 127, 130
Stirling Journal, 15
Stock Exchange Securities, 17, 131,
  132
Stockport, 38
Strathaven, 15
  and radical politics, 22–3
Strathaven Radicals, 22
Sybil, 37

Tariff protection
  see Import duties
Tariff Reformers, 51

Taxation of the poor, 88
Tenements, 80
Thornton, W.T., 37, 38
Times, The, 17, 19, 20, 21, 40, 51,
  91, 133
Trade cycles, 35
Truck system, 74
Tyneside, 103

Ulster, 37
Unionist Party, 50, 51
Utility theory, 59
  see also Value and utility, Money

Valpy, Richard, 18
Value and utility, 5, 53, 54, 55, 56,
  109, 111
Vandermeulen, D.C., 123, 124

Wales
  diet in, 71
  South, 103
Walker, D.A., 126
Ward, Thomas, 40
Welsh labourers, living standards
  of, 37
Westminster Gazette, 6
Wheat
  consumption of, 6, 7, 10, 11,
  72–3
demand for, 111
elasticity of demand for, 6, 11
English, 72
imports, 61
imports and bread prices, 27
price of, 10, 30, 31, 63, 98
tax on imports of, 6
Whitechapel, 79, 80
  bread consumption in, 85, 86
  paradox in, 86, 87, 92
Wigan, 105
Wikan, U., 136
Wilson, James, 22
Wood, Margaret Ann, 19
Working class
  diet of, 33, 34